DO NOT REMOVE
CARDS FROM POCKET

DAY CARE

Looking for Answers

Kathlyn Gay

—Issues in Focus—

ENSLOW PUBLISHERS, INC.

Bloy St. and Ramsey Ave.
Box 777
Hillside, N.J. 07205
U.S.A.

P.O. Box 38
Aldershot
Hants GU12 6BP
U.K.

Library of Congress Cataloging-in-Publication Data

Gay, Kathlyn.
    Day care: looking for answers / Kathlyn Gay.
       p. cm. — (Issues in focus)
    Includes bibliographical references and index.
    Summary: Describes the contemporary day care industry, its
benefits, and drawbacks, the alternatives available to parents, and actions being
taken by government and corporations.
    ISBN 0-89490-324-1
    1. Day care centers—United States—Juvenile literature. 2. Child
care services—United States—Juvenile literature. [1. Day care
centers.] I. Title II. Series: Issues in focus (Hillside, N.J.)
HV854.G39   1992
362.7'12'0973—dc20   91-18141
                                         CIP
                                         AC

Printed in the United States of America

10 9 8 7 6 5 4 3 2 1

Illustration Credits:
Betterae McIntyre, pp. 49, 93; Doris Kimmel, pp. 30, 40, 47; Kathlyn Gay, pp. 4,
35, 42, 56, 63 (bottom), 65, 76, 87, 108; Martin Gay, p. 63 (top); New Jersey
Department of Community Affairs, p. 90

Cover Photo:
photo by James Karales/Peter Arnold, Inc.

Contents

1

The Need for Child Care

Margaret rushes to bundle up her three-month-old son, Jason. She grabs a bag with diapers and bottles, stuffs in several textbooks, and hurries out of her home to catch the school bus at the corner. Margaret is on her way to a midwestern high school that has set up a center where teenage parents can leave their children while their mothers attend classes during the day.

It's 7:00 A.M., and Ben and Ivory are out the door of their suburban home near Dallas, Texas, with two preschool boys in tow. On the way to his office, Ben will drop Ivory off at the bank where she works and then head for the day-care center. Both of the boys have been going to the center ever since they were a few months old.

Rita and Ken work a family farm in Minnesota, and Ken also holds a part-time job selling farm machinery. Rita handles many of the farm chores and would like to be able to find day care for five-year-old Janice who is hearing-impaired and in a wheelchair. Although one day-care center, out of the dozens they contacted, would accept their daughter, they would have to drive thirty miles to get her there.

5

It was a "miracle," according to Donella. She and her two children had been homeless for months and were living in the temporary house set up by a downtown church. The "miracle" was the fact that church members had decided to open a day-care center where homeless children could stay while their parents looked for work and permanent places to live.

Every day in the United States, millions of adults from all walks of life struggle with the dilemma of caring for dependent children. The question "Who will care for the children?" frequently demands a search for a caregiver and also raises other questions about the kinds of care a child will receive and about the affordability of that care. Some of the problems facing families have come about because of changes in the work force and in family structures. Increasing poverty rates also play a role in child-care problems.

The Changing Work Force

Until World War II, it was traditional for women to care for their children and often older parents or disabled family members in the home. But when men joined the armed forces, women were needed for factory work and other types of labor.

After the war, men again were the primary wage earners while many women returned to homemaking. This idealized type of family was frequently described in print and pictured in electronic media during the 1950s and still is considered the model family structure by many Americans. However, it was a model that fit primarily white middle-class families. Other families, particularly immigrant and minority, have depended for survival on the wages of both parents and frequently the minor children. Until recent times, it was common for all members of a rural family who were physically able to work on the farm or at a craft.

Since the 1960s, an increasing number of women have demanded equality in the nation's social, political, and economic arenas, and the roles of women have changed greatly. Many are holding jobs once considered traditional male occupations—from trucker to telephone repair person to engineer to scientist. Only 18 percent of all American families function like the family of yesteryear, with the husband as breadwinner and the wife as homemaker.

Today, the number of women in the labor force has increased dramatically. At least 52 million women—more than half of the women in the United States—work outside the home, compared to about 20 percent a century ago. At present, over 70 percent of all mothers with children between the ages of six and seventeen work outside the home. By 1995, about 15 million preschool children (under the age of six) will have mothers in the labor force, according to a researcher with The Urban Institute in Washington, D.C.[1]

Although some women are in the work force because they choose to be there, at least two-thirds of the women who work at paid jobs do so because they must help support their families or are the sole breadwinners. In many cases, the family income is under $15,000 a year.

Changes in the work force also are a reflection of changes in the number of Americans in the labor pool. During the so-called baby boom years of the 1950s, birth rates were high, and that generation provided a surplus of workers through the 1970s and into the 1980s. But birth rates have fallen since the boom years, and many businesses and industries are facing worker shortages, which in turn mean that more women will be needed to fill future job openings. Many of these women will be mothers, so there will be an even larger need for care outside the home for children and other dependent family members. The U.S. Labor Department predicts that by the year 2000, the parents of more than 80 percent of American school-age children and 70 percent of preschoolers will be working outside the home.

Other Factors

Another factor that contributes to the increasing need for child care is the divorce rate. Divorces per every thousand marriages have almost tripled since the end of World War II. There also has been an increase in the number of unmarried teenage mothers who are raising their children. (In earlier times, because of the stigma against unmarried mothers, women who bore children out of wedlock often released their babies for adoption by married couples.)

The demand for professional (paid) caregivers is also related in part to the lack of supportive family networks, a situation that is quite different from what it was several generations ago. During the early 1900s, most families lived in closely knit communities, either in small towns or urban neighborhoods with extended family members—grandparents, aunts, uncles, and cousins—and friends nearby. People stayed within a community most of their lives and frequently provided services for one another, such as helping to care for children, the sick, or the elderly. Today, however, families are more mobile. Many move away from places where they were born, leaving the people who could be counted on for various types of support. Without the network of helping hands, families turn to professionals for child care and other services needed for disabled family members—if such services are available and affordable.

Poverty Compounds Problems

Other social and economic conditions have pushed child-care problems to the crisis level. For example, many experts on family issues believe that some of the problems are related to the fact that a great number of households are headed by a person who works full time at the minimum wage, earning about $9,000 annually. After paying for such basics as food and shelter, there is little or nothing left for health and child care.

Federal programs designed to help poor families meet basic needs were cut during the 1980s. The administration of President Ronald Reagan was strongly opposed to federal funding for many social programs, believing that state governments, businesses, and volunteers should support such efforts. But adequate funds for family programs did not materialize. Thus, the number of poor families increased, adding to the difficulties of caring for children.

Children make up the largest group of poor in the United States. The child poverty rate is more than double what it is in other industrialized nations such as Great Britain, Germany, and Sweden. These countries provide aid for families, including funds for housing, as well as programs for job training, health care, and child care.

Because many American children lack proper health care and nutrition, they suffer mental and physical disabilities and serious illnesses. Even before birth, a child's health is endangered if the mother does not get medical care or nutritious food. Malnutrition can lead to serious mental disabilities and physical problems for an infant or even cause death. The infant mortality rate in the United States is worse than that of many developing countries, ranking twentieth in the world.[2]

Poverty also leads to homelessness. According to statistics published in a special edition of *Newsweek,* 33 million Americans are poor. Thirteen million of the poor are children, and 500,000 of those children are homeless.[3]

Some homeless families find refuge for a time in crowded shelters or stay in parks or abandoned buildings or live in cars. Certainly homelessness affects a child's health, education, and sometimes the ability later in life to be a self-sustaining individual.

"The lives of homeless children tell us much of the disregard that society has shown for vulnerable people," wrote Jonathan Kozol, the author of a number of books on the plight of America's children. As Kozol points out:

> Many of these kids grow up surrounded by infectious illnesses no longer seen in most developed nations. Whooping cough and tuberculosis . . . are now familiar in the shelters. Shocking numbers of these children have not been inoculated and for this reason cannot go to school. Those who do are likely to be two years behind grade level.[4]

Even when parents are able to provide the basic necessities such as shelter, food, and clothing, they may be unable to stretch limited incomes to pay for child care. Parents may have no relatives or friends nearby to care for their children. As a result, up to seven million children stay home alone after school. At the age of eleven or twelve, most children are able to take some responsibility for their own care for a few hours. But many children much younger are on their own. In the Washington, D.C., area, at least 15 percent of the children between eight and ten years old take care of themselves after school while their parents work, according to a *Washington Post* poll.[5]

Because "latchkey kids," as they have been called, are not supervised, they may be victims of household fires, poisonings, or other hazards. In many parts of the nation, volunteer hotline programs for latchkey children have been set up to handle emergency calls and also calls from children who feel lonely or frightened or just need a friendly person to talk to when they are home alone. Volunteers also visit schools to advise children on how to handle situations such as being locked out of the home or encountering strangers.

Still, as child-care experts have frequently noted, much more needs to be done to deal with the problem of caring for growing numbers of latchkey children. But who will set up the services and pay the costs? That is only one of many questions about child-care needs.

More Questions About Needs

Along with trying to find services that are affordable, parents ask what kind of care is appropriate. What facilities are available? Do caregivers provide quality care?

Many parents also agonize over whether their children will suffer adverse effects by spending hours each day with caregivers other than themselves. Parents struggle with such issues as whether they will be able to take an extended work leave to stay home with an infant or sick child (or other dependent family member); they worry about surviving without a paycheck or losing their jobs. Some families are concerned about the lack of day care for disabled members. Others want to know how school-age children should be cared for while parents are on the job.

These are some of the questions that will be discussed in the chapters that follow. But you will find no simple answers. Each of the dependent care issues involves pros and cons. Many debates concern so-called family values, which are based on differences in the way people view the family and who the caregivers should be.

2

Debating the Issues

"Who *should* care for kids?" That is one of the most controversial questions raised in the discussions about child care in the United States. One side says flatly: "Parents should be responsible for their own children. Period." Others argue that government funds should be provided to help working parents pay for quality child care by a caregiver in or out of a child's home.

But the debate over the public role in child care is more complex than whether or not government should fund the care of children. There are those who argue that child care in nurseries or preschools help children from all walks of life in their social and intellectual development. Others disagree, saying that child care should be primarily for children who may otherwise be neglected. Such arguments have been going on in the United States for nearly two centuries, ever since the first "day nurseries" were established in growing industrial areas.

Early Day Nurseries

Some of the first day nurseries in the United States were patterned after infant schools established in France and Britain during the 1800s. The European schools cared for children of mothers who worked outside the home in factories that were rapidly increasing in number. Similar nurseries appeared in the United States—the Boston Infant School, for example, opened in 1828 and served children eighteen months old to four years of age. Its main purpose was to help working mothers by easing some of their "domestic cares," which in turn would "enable them to seek employment." [1]

In other cities, infant schools and nurseries were set up for the same reason—to care for children of working parents, many of whom were poor immigrants trying to find jobs in the industries of growing urban centers. Millions (1.2 million in New York City alone) lived in crowded tenements, wooden structures several stories high that lacked sanitary facilities, were infested with vermin, and often were labeled "human pigsties." Conditions were seldom better in factories that had little ventilation and few if any safety precautions.

Charity workers and educators of the period were concerned about the effects of poverty on children. Since some children from the slums turned to crime as a means of survival, it was commonly believed that poor children would automatically become criminals. In efforts to protect society, neglected children sometimes were rounded up from the streets of eastern cities and sent to foster homes, orphanages, or farms in the Midwest, where they worked as servants.[2]

By the end of the 1800s, social reformers were stressing the need for better care of poor children, and day nurseries were thought to be one of the best alternatives to "ideal" family life—that is, the father providing income and the mother caring for children. Some reformers believed that nurseries provided far healthier living conditions for infants and toddlers than tenement family life, particularly if the father had died, was ill, or had abandoned the family.

Caregivers were primarily concerned about keeping children, clean and away from the dangers and evil influences of the streets. They also wanted to help mothers find work so they could improve their lives. Yet because most day nurseries were not inspected or professionally staffed, some were probably as unsanitary as the tenements and no more than warehouses for holding young children until they could be released to their parents.

About the time day nurseries were introduced in the United States, ideas about the education of young children were also gaining attention. Some educators in Europe began to organize kindergartens and nurseries that provided programs to help children in their social and physical development and learning skills. Organized play, singing, story reading, and other activities were part of the daily routine. As these ideas spread to the United States, some nurseries incorporated educational programs for the young children in their care, and kindergartens and preschools were established.

Through the late 1800s and early 1900s, social work also became established as a profession. Like many professional caregivers of that time, social workers for the most part saw care of children outside the home as a symptom of a family in trouble. Families who needed child care were considered "maladjusted"—unable to function in a healthy or positive manner—so the main goal was to help mothers stay at home and care for their children. If that was not possible, it was believed that children would be better off with relatives or with a foster family. Such beliefs prompted the idea that care for children in a day-care center was only for "problem families"—families who needed welfare services.[3]

In some communities, the stigma of day care as welfare still exists, even though many affluent and middle-income families place their children in a variety of facilities that provide day care but may be labeled differently. In fact, day care has become an important part of some families' support systems, no longer provided by extended family members or a closely knit community.

Continued Debate Over "Woman's Place"

Although the roles of women have changed greatly over the past four decades, many Americans (as well as people in other nations) still believe that a woman's "proper place" is in the home, caring for children and doing housework. Of course, as an increasing number of women have entered the labor force, many more men are helping with child care and household tasks than they did even a decade ago. But as survey after survey shows, women who work outside the home frequently do double duty—besides holding a paid job, women still do most of the housework and parenting, working at least fifteen hours more per week than men.

The idea of "woman's place" is partly responsible for the fact that women who have children are less likely to rise to executive positions than those who are childless. If mothers cannot find quality child care, they may drop out of a high-pressure work schedule and opt for part-time work at a lower pay rate. Again, this is the case for some fathers, but the majority of fathers who are in executive positions or working toward promotions are not expected to assume child-care responsibilities. In fact, even when fathers are allowed to take paternity leave from their jobs to help care for a newborn, many prefer instead to take "sick leave" or vacation time. The image of being a caregiver is considered "too feminine" (meaning "soft") for men who see themselves as "macho" (tough guys), although there are indications that for some men at least these stereotypical roles are changing.

Those who believe in traditional family roles frequently argue that government programs supporting child care allow women to give higher priorities to jobs than to family life. As a professor of philosophy at Chicago's DePaul University wrote:

> If one chooses the possibility of motherhood . . . one must accept the full responsibilities. That means personally to love, nurture, and provide for that child and not to shove those responsibilities

16

onto others because working outside the home is less tedious and less boring than changing diapers and feeding little mouths . . .[4]

That point of view, however, is not shared by many working mothers who say that boredom has nothing to do with working outside the home; they must hold jobs to pay the expenses of rearing children. Indeed, a *New York Times* poll of nearly 1,500 parents found that of the working women surveyed, "24 percent said they worked to support themselves, 36 percent to support their family, 27 percent for extra money and [only] 9 percent for 'something interesting to do.' " A factory worker in Missouri told a pollster that she would rather stay home with her three kids but "It takes two incomes" to cover her family's expenses, noting that "Half of my paycheck and sometimes all of it goes to the grocery store." [5]

A study for the U.S. Congress' Joint Economic Committee found that family income has declined since the 1970s. Families need two wage earners just to stay even, and those with only one wage earner show a decline in income, the congressional report noted.

Should Government Support Child Care?

For the past few years, national surveys and polls have shown that an increasing number of Americans believe that the nation's children are precious resources about which everyone should be concerned. As Sandra L. Hofferth, a researcher at The Urban Institute who prepared a report for Congress on child-care needs, put it:

> . . . the root of the [child care] problem has still to be addressed: our society's devaluation of childbearing and childrearing. There is little reward for caring for children, whether as a parent or child care provider. Even pediatricians earn less for their work than specialists with older individuals. We must, as a society, place greater importance on providing and paying for high-quality services for children . . .[6]

One nationwide survey on child-care issues was conducted by twenty-one major consumer magazines, including *People, New*

17

Republic, Changing Times, Cosmopolitan, and *Parents.* During the survey, which elicited some 200,000 responses, a majority of women who did not work outside the home and women without children indicated that they believed the federal government should give top priority to family concerns, as did half of the men who responded. Asked whether a worker had the right to take a leave from a job to care for a newborn or seriously ill dependent, 93 percent responded "yes." The survey also showed that 65 percent felt the government should help make child care more affordable for all families and set standards for child-care facilities.

Those ideas are now new. Ever since the end of World War II, advocates for improvements in America's child-care programs have been trying to present their case to federal legislators. In 1971, Congress passed the Comprehensive Child Development Act, which would have made day care available free to people receiving welfare payments and would have allowed middle-income families to pay a graduated fee for child-care services depending on earnings. But President Richard Nixon vetoed the bill saying that government-supported child care would be similar to "communal approaches to child-rearing over against the family-centered approach." He was supported by some members of Congress and other Americans who believed free child care was part of a plot to turn America into a communistic or socialistic system.

Through the 1980s, many Americans continued to oppose government intervention in child care, claiming it posed a threat to families and would encourage more mothers to work. Federally supported child care, some believed, would discriminate against those parents who stay home to care for their children or have relatives who provide child care at little or no cost. They feared that the federal government would try to impose regulations on informal child-care arrangements with baby-sitters and neighbors. Others claimed that teachers needed jobs, so they were pushing for government support of day-care centers.

In spite of opposition, the demand for some type of federal leadership in child-care issues did not go away. As many advocates for children have pointed out, the United States is the only industrialized nation other than South Africa that has no federal policy or comprehensive guidelines for child care. Only recently has the U.S. government taken beginning steps toward a national child-care policy.

Sheila B. Kamerman of the Columbia University School of Social Work took a look at child-care services on an international basis. She found that other nations have established policies that permit working parents, whether biological or adoptive, some time off to care for a newborn without losing employment or income. "The only differences among the countries have to do with the length of the leave, the level of the benefit, and the inclusion of fathers as well as mothers," Kamerman noted.[7]

In Scandinavian and some other European nations and in Japan, both government and industry support child-care programs. For many years, Swedish laws have required that parents receive 90 percent of their earnings when they are on leave from their jobs to care for newborns. Either parent (mother or father) receives her or his earnings for twelve months and then can work a six-hour day until the child is eight years old. German women may take fourteen weeks of maternity leave at full salary, and either parent can take sixteen months of additional leave with reduced earnings. Japanese women receive six weeks leave before their children are born and another eight weeks to care for their newborns at home. During their leave time, they receive 60 percent of their basic pay.

When European children get beyond the infant and toddler stage, they are frequently cared for in government-funded nurseries or preschools. Day care is treated as a form of education. According to *U.S. News & World Report:*

> In France and Belgium, 95 percent of 3-to-5-year-olds are in primary school for up to 9 hours a day; in Italy and Denmark, the proportion is almost as high . . . [In] Britain and Ireland, half the preschoolers attend state-run child-care facilities.[8]

A U.S. delegation of fourteen professionals from diverse fields (including business, medicine, and labor) spent two weeks in 1989 studying France's child-care system. In a report on its findings, the delegation said that France was "far ahead" of the United States "in insuring that its young children are well and safely cared for." French child-care workers must be college educated and trained in early childhood development. Those who care for infants and toddlers must have public health training, and directors of programs for those under three years of age are nurses or midwives. In contrast, most American child-care workers are not required to obtain a college education or special training, although administrators in many child-care facilities are setting up programs to encourage employees to further their education.

American experts found broad political support for government-subsidized child care in France and noted that 49 percent of a person's income is spent on taxes compared to 31 percent in the United States. Yet some drawbacks were reported, such as the strict centralized control of the child-care system in France. The U.S. system provides for more local and state controls.

Recent U.S. Legislative Actions

During his election campaign in 1988, President George Bush noted that child care was "the single most important issue arising from the changes in our work force." He vowed to get the country "working together to reach our children." [9]

However, in 1990, President Bush vetoed legislation that would have required companies with over fifty employees to provide up to twelve weeks of unpaid leave to workers who take time off for a serious illness or to care for infants or other dependent family members. The proposed law also required employers to guarantee workers their jobs or equivalent positions when they returned to work and to continue any health insurance benefits previously provided.

Many businesses were opposed to such legislation, fearing that they soon would be required to provide paid leaves. The Bush administration argued that the federal government should not determine company policies and that businesses should determine the types of family benefits to offer. Meantime, however, a number of states—Maine, Connecticut, Maryland, New Jersey, and Wisconsin among them—have passed laws of their own requiring companies to offer their employees leave time to care for family members.

Controversy also surrounded laws that would provide federal funds (called block grants) to states for programs to improve child-care facilities. Bush opposed such measures, fearing that block grants would lead to a huge federal bureaucracy to operate the program. His administration wanted to limit child care primarily to expanded tax credits—low-income families would be able to deduct from federal income taxes larger amounts than previously allowed for child-care expenses.

After much debate, however, federal legislation to address child-care needs was passed in late 1990, the first such measure to be approved since World War II. The legislation allows expanded tax credits and also provides grants to states. States may use 75 percent of their grant to directly aid low-income families who need child-care services or to increase the number and to improve the quality of child-care facilities. Child-care providers who receive funds must meet health and safety standards.

The federal legislation requires that some of the remaining grant money be spent to set up school programs to serve latchkey children. In addition, some funds must be used to provide training for caregivers or to increase the pay for workers in child-care facilities.[10]

Members of Congress who sponsored the child-care legislation and representatives of many child-care organizations believe more funding is needed. But they are hopeful that the legislation will be a base for future programs to improve child care in the nation.

3

The Caregivers

In spite of the fact that millions of children are cared for outside their homes while their parents are working, many youngsters still are cared for in their *own* homes. Relatives—grandparents, aunts, uncles, cousins, or other extended family members—may be the caregivers. In some cases, parents set up offices or home businesses so they can care for their children at home and at the same time earn income.

When parents need professional caregivers—those who are paid for their services—they may want their children to be cared for in their own homes by nonrelatives who either live in or come to the home on a regular basis. Options for care outside a child's own home may include facilities such as a family day-care home, a day-care center, or a nursery.

In some parts of the country, however, there is a short supply of *regulated* services, due in part to "mismatches between the ages of children needing care and the kinds of services available," say researchers at The Urban Institute in Washington, D.C.[1] In other words, even if parents can find child care, the quality might not meet their standards or be what they want or need. Or the available child care might not be affordable.

Professional Nannies

The majority of parents would prefer to have a qualified caregiver come into their home to care for their children. That caregiver could be a baby-sitter, a housekeeper, or a professionally trained nursemaid, frequently called a nanny, who lives with a family.

Usually, such services are more expensive than family day care or child-care centers. In most urban areas, for example, live-in nannies are paid $200 to $300 per week. The range in Denver and Dallas is $200 to $350 and in New York can go from $225 to as high as $500 per week. But among young couples who are advancing in well-paid careers (often referred to as Yuppies), there has been an increasing demand for professional nannies.

At least 75,000 nannies are providing child care in homes across the nation, according to Cathie Robertson, president of the International Nanny Association. Robertson, who also trains nannies at Grossmont Community College near San Diego, California, says that "we can't possibly fill the demand" because for every trained nanny there are 25 to 250 families offering a position.[2]

A similar type of live-in arrangement involves *au pairs,* young people from other countries who come to the United States to serve as nursemaids. The young men and women are between eighteen and twenty-five years old and receive visas to live with an American family for a year, working forty-five hours per week, according to a report in *Money* magazine. To qualify for the visas, the young people must be fluent in English, have a secondary-school education, and be experienced in child care. American families pay the air fare, health insurance, and similar costs plus about $100 per week allowance for au pairs.[3]

Family Day Care

> Child care in my home. Educated
> mother. Fenced yard. Playroom.

Such an ad might be found in the classified section of a newspaper or tacked on a bulletin board in an apartment complex or community laundromat. When parents are looking for affordable child care, they frequently turn to family day care in their own or nearby neighborhood. Although there are a number of definitions for family day care, it usually involves one provider caring for several children.

Typically a woman may start a family day-care service because it is a way to earn income at home, and if she has children, she can care for them as well as others. For example, an Evanston, Illinois, mother who is also a pediatric nurse cares for two infants plus her own two children. She prefers caring for babies but must charge at least $125 per week in order to earn enough to work at home rather than in a medical office or hospital. In a Pennsylvania community, a former teacher provides care for preschoolers, offering programs that parents say promote their children's educational and social development. A Texas woman who once operated a day-care center now provides family day care for six children—an infant, two toddlers, and three preschoolers.

About half of all preschool children in out-of-home care are placed in family day-care homes, according to a nationwide study recently released by the Children's Defense Fund (CDF), a national organization working to protect children and to improve their lives. Parents report that one of the reasons they choose family day care is because of the home setting, which they hope will allow more individual attention and personal care for their children. As one mother explained:

> I feel really lucky to have Bernice [a day-care provider] in our
> neighborhood. She is like my son's second mom, and the other
> kids Bernice cares for feel the same way. But Bernice doesn't do

25

things in a haphazard way. She is very organized and provides learning opportunities for the kids as well as letting them have time to just do their own thing.[4]

Another major benefit of a family day-care arrangement is continuity. A person who provides care on a continual basis offers stability and allows a very young child to form attachments and feel secure. In contrast, because of low wages, there may be a huge turnover of employees—teachers and aides—in a day-care center.

Flexibility, many parents say, is another plus. Hours of care may vary according to the needs of families. Providers may care for children with minor illnesses and may take infants under three months of age, which usually is not the case with day-care centers.

Costs for family day care may be less also. Centers must pass on overhead charges, such as the costs of worker salaries and building maintenance. But family day-care providers usually do not have the large expenditures of most day-care centers and may be able to adjust their charges to fit what parents can afford to pay.

Are there drawbacks to family day care? Lax regulation is one of the most serious concerns. In just one metropolitan area—Philadelphia—some 1,700 homes are registered with the state of Pennsylvania for day care. But officials believe anywhere from 6,500 to 8,500 additional homes are operating without a license. Similar situations exist in other states, and family day-care providers may operate for years without a license unless an accident or hazardous condition calls public attention to the home.

A recent news story, for example, described how a Maryland woman, Nannie Pressley, was providing child care for twenty children in her home, which was well kept but not licensed for child care. At the time authorities inspected her home, they found fifty-four children, thirteen of them infants, under the temporary supervision of Pressley's teenage daughter. Pressley told reporters that most of the children were guests for a birthday party and that she had gone to a nearby store to buy supplies for the party.

Most of Pressley's neighbors described her as a caring person and someone on whom young working mothers depended—she often cared for infants of single mothers who could not afford day care in a center. Maryland authorities pointed out that state regulations limit home care to six children but that many unlicensed homes are operating because there is such a dire need for affordable child care.

CDF estimates that 75 percent of the preschool children in family day care across the nation "are in homes exempt from state licensing, a fact all the more alarming since infants and toddlers, the most vulnerable of young children, are more often cared for in family day-care homes than in child-care centers." Yet CDF expects that the recently passed federal child-care measure will bring some improvements. States will receive funds needed to help providers improve the quality of their facilities and at the same time maintain affordable rates for low-income families.[5]

There are other problems, however. Even if providers obtain state licenses for family day care, some local zoning laws define family day care as a business, which is prohibited in residential areas. People fear that setting up day care in a residential neighborhood will lead other service businesses to operate in a residential zone. In fact, the *Philadelphia Inquirer* reported that suburban communities "have become a battleground between family day-care operators, who say they are providing a valuable service, and [those who] view day care as a nuisance." [6]

Some Pennsylvania communities allow family day care if providers obtain an exemption to a zoning ordinance and pay the cost of a permit. But most providers feel they cannot afford such fees. In Pennsylvania, as well as in other states, family day-care providers have filed legal suits to appeal zoning decisions, arguing successfully that communities should not deny caregivers when the state issues licenses for and regulates the homes.

One family day-care provider who had been licensed by the state of California had been providing care for seven years but in 1989 was denied a city permit to operate. Her home was on a dead-end street, which the planning director said did not allow easy access for emergency vehicles trying to get to the area. But with the support of state officials who appeared at a special hearing on the issue, the local planning commission reversed the director's decision. In 1990, the provider received a special-use permit for her family day-care service.

Along with local variations in day-care licensing and permits, state regulations and standards also vary greatly. In Massachusetts, where more than 9,000 homes are licensed for day care, a provider is allowed to care for up to six children. Other states may allow up to ten children in a home. Virginia does not require a state license for home providers who care for less than six children, although some county governments in the state regulate anyone who provides child care for a full day.

In some states, providers, who must be at least eighteen years old, are required to obtain health certificates showing they are free of communicable diseases and tuberculosis. Providers may be required to get training in emergency first aid. Regulations also may cover fire safety in the home and inspections for lead-free paint.

Recently some state officials have called for much broader and stricter regulations for family day-care homes. In Maryland, for example, state legislators have proposed that all adults living in a home providing day care be fingerprinted and checked for criminal records. Other proposals have included requirements that caregivers get training in child development, keep detailed records of children they care for, and in short, operate as a business rather than as a loose familylike structure.

Parents looking for family day care may want to check whether the home has a state license or has been registered with a local governmental agency. The National Association for Family Day Care certifies family day-care homes and provides information on those that have been accredited by the association.

Advice on what to look for in day-care providers has been included in the many recent articles published in major magazines and newspapers (see **Further Reading**). The final chapter of this book includes a summary of some of the guidelines for choosing day care.

Day-Care Centers

Although family day-care homes have been in the spotlight on occasion in recent years, most of the public attention on out-of-home care has focused on day-care centers for preschool children. Centers may be operated as a business (for profit) or set up as nonprofit organizations. Increasingly, large corporations and small companies also are setting up day-care centers for children of employees. Some special centers for sick children, the disabled, the homeless, and for combined care of the elderly and children also are available but not in any great number.

For-profit centers are part of what is expected to be a $48 billion industry in the United States by 1995.[7] Some of these are national chains like Busy Bee, LaPetite Academy, Children's World, and Kinder-Care, which serve a broad age range of children.

Kinder-Care is by far the largest day-care operation in the United States. The multimillion dollar business originated in Montgomery, Alabama, in 1969. It now has more than 1,200 centers located in most of the states and in Canada. The company plans to build several hundred more before the end of the 1990s. At most locations there are long waiting lists, particularly for infant care.

Perhaps the most important factor in Kinder-Care's financial success is its standardization—rather like the McDonald's or the Holiday Inn of child care. People know what to expect wherever a center is located. Every facility is basically alike, from the layout of buildings (with a bell tower on top) to furniture to day-by-day schedules and programs.

Yet there are critics of this homogenized, mass-marketed kind of care. Some say that although physical surroundings are uniform, the quality of a center varies from location to location. Kinder-Care and other chains follow standards set by each state or local government, which means that there are broad differences in the type of training and education required for caregivers. There are also variations in the ratio of teachers to students. For example, one state may require a

Art projects are part of the daily routine in an on-site day-care center in Portland, Oregon.

teacher for every six three-year-olds; another may allow up to twelve per teacher. As in other day-care facilities, turnover rates for teachers and workers may be high because of low wages. However, the chain operations are able to offer some employee benefits, such as insurance programs and opportunities for advancement, that are not always available at smaller day-care facilities.

Although national child-care chains enjoy name recognition and are increasing in popularity, many other for-profit child-care centers are providing services without much fanfare. Some are regional operations. Creative World of Child Care, Inc., of Huber Heights, Ohio, is an example. Initiated in 1975 by Martha Lampe, who has a graduate degree in business administration, Creative World took over from a bankrupt company that had hoped to establish a national chain. The Ohio company includes eight centers that serve over 800 children in the greater Dayton and Springfield areas, including school-age children who are transported to and from their schools.

In an interview for *Child Care Information Exchange,* Lampe pointed out that many day-care providers "serve the most profitable" groups needing child care—the suburban preschoolers. "To keep our centers in business we have had to modify and service the more difficult, labor intensive infant and toddler market, expand flexible schedules, and develop latchkey programs," she said.

Other private child-care centers serve metropolitan areas. One is Quality Time Early Learning Center in Silver Spring, Maryland. Located in the metropolitan area near Washington, D.C., Quality Time opened in 1989 in a refurbished four-story factory, renovated at a cost of $1.4 million. A bright, airy facility, the center includes classrooms, a music room, computer center, all-purpose room, cafeteria, and of course toys and books appropriate for the age groups served. "The center has enrolled 170 youngsters but can accommodate about 199, from infants to school-age children," says Marian Brooks, one of the center administrators. "We hire staff trained in early childhood development and also provide a training program for teachers and aides. It is the kind of day care environment that is truly designed to be a model facility," she says.[8]

In order to establish such a center, an investor, Richard Crump, raised money through private loans and liens on real estate, plus loans secured by Maryland's Day Care Facilities Loan Guarantee Fund Program. The fund guarantees payment of 80 percent of a loan from a bank or other lending institution. Since 1984, the Maryland loan program has been the impetus for lending agencies to loan $2.2 million for twenty-two child-care centers in the state. The program not only helps get new centers started but also allows existing centers to make improvements.

Some centers set up as business operations are fairly small, enrolling only thirty or forty children in contrast to a large center that may have a capacity for one hundred children or more. One small child-care center called Creative Beginnings was initiated a few years ago by a businessman in Bremen, Indiana. The operation has yet to actually show a profit, but the owner said his primary purpose for the center was to fill a need and "to give something back to the community."

A great variety of child-care centers are set up as nonprofit organizations. In other words, they are not designed to provide a profit for the owners, but instead are set up so that fees for services, donations, and grants will cover costs. Government funds help subsidize the costs of such child care for families who otherwise could not afford the services.

Some nonprofit centers have been operating successfully ever since the late 1800s. Consider the Lincoln Day Nursery in South Philadelphia. It has been in operation for more than one hundred years and provides daily care for children three to nine years of age. Since most families in the neighborhood cannot afford the fee of $70 per week per child, the center receives federal subsidies to operate. Parents pay from $5 to $20 per week for a child's care, depending on the family's income.

The center does not get much publicity outside its own neighborhood, but many families depend on it for their survival. Without it, many parents would not be able to hold jobs, or their children would be forced to stay home alone while their parents worked. One mother whose two children are enrolled at Lincoln says, "I honestly don't know what I would do without [the center] ... it's like having second parents away from home." She also notes that her children have learned a lot at the center and that the staff encourages parents to visit. "You can spend all the time you want with the kids," she says.[9]

Some nonprofit nursery schools or day-care centers operate as cooperatives (coops), an idea that apparently originated in Europe and has become popular in California, where there are about 400 coop nurseries. Most parent-run coops lease space in a church or community building and set up a child-care program with professional caregivers. The cost, which is determined by the number of days a child attends the program, ranges from about $50 to $100 a month. Parents take turns helping with activities. For example, at a Pasadena, California, nursery, one father took time off from his job as a financial planner to do his share of the coop duties. Along with four other parents, he helped mop floors and prepare snacks and served as a teacher aide.

Although local groups operate most nonprofit day-care centers, some national organizations are involved in providing nonprofit child care. The YWCA of the USA is one. According to the executive director, "More than half of YWCAs around the country have fully-licensed, professionally staffed child-care centers. Many are designed to meet the developmental needs of infants to older children" and include after-school programs for latchkey children and day-camp facilities. However, like many other nonprofit day-care centers, the YWCA must continually seek funds to support its services.[10]

Overcoming Day-Care Problems

While some child-care centers struggle to stay financially sound, other issues also concern providers. One of the most troublesome is the possibility of being falsely accused of child abuse. Because of the widespread and sensational news coverage of several notorious sexual abuse cases in day-care centers (as well as in private homes), some parents are quick to allege abuse on the basis of rumors. Yet several studies show that abuse in child-care centers is rare.

In a three-year study by the Family Research Laboratory at the University of New Hampshire, researchers found that most child abuse occurs in children's own homes, and very few children are abused by professional caregivers. Still, once a child-care provider has been accused, the accusation sticks—even when no evidence supports the charge. To avoid false allegations and protect their reputations, many day-care providers expend much time and effort to keep communication lines open with parents and others in their communities.

Another major problem facing child-care centers across the nation is the 41 percent turnover rate of staff. "It's backbreaking work, the hours are long, and the stress sometimes seems intolerable. On top of that, the pay is awful, and nobody respects what you do. So why do it?" a teacher at a day-care center asked recently after an especially difficult day. The teacher answered her rhetorical question by pointing out that she, like many others in the profession, are caregivers because they love children and find many rewards in child-care work in spite of minimal wages.

According to a report from the Child Care Employees Project, a research group at Berkeley, California, teachers in day-care centers earn far less than the average American worker— 40 to 60 percent less. Aides who earn the lowest income (sometimes below the poverty level) make better wages at entry-level jobs in fast-food restaurants or similar places of employment. Not only are wages low, but there are few if any benefits such as insurance for child-care aides.

Because of low wages, child-care teachers may leave the profession for better paying jobs, but it is not unusual for teachers to return to the work they love. One young woman at an Illinois child-care center left to become a secretary at a salary almost double what she earned as a child-care teacher. However, she returned because she said the money was not what made her happy; working with young children did.

Kim Peckwas, another Illinois child-care professional, shares that view. Peckwas, who has a bachelor's degree in child development and a master's degree in education, is co-director of a nursery school in Chicago, earning about $15,000 per year. She was among ten child-care workers from across the nation to be honored in 1990 for excellence and achievement. After accepting her $1,000 award presented by the National Child Care Association and Hardee's

Although pay for child care providers is low (not more than $5.00 per hour for certified workers), this provider finds great personal satisfaction working in a day-care center.

restaurant chain, Peckwas explained how uplifting it can be to work with youngsters and to be a recipient of their affection. "You can be tired and crabby and not feeling good, and one of the kids will run up and grab your leg, and say, 'Miss Kimmy,' and it makes you feel better. It really does," she said.[11]

Another drawback for many day-care professionals who are college graduates trained in early childhood development is the fact that they are frequently perceived as "baby-sitters"—merely watching children, not contributing to their growth. Unfortunately, the lack of respect for child-care workers reflects a common view among Americans that caring for children is a job anyone can do. Directors of day-care programs know this is not the case. Over and over again they point out that quality caregivers must be able to relate to children and also know what children need at their various stages of development. One director explained:

> Day-care teachers provide experiences to stimulate learning in all developmental areas—emotional, intellectual, physical, and social. They encourage children's natural curiosity and activities. Most importantly, they see each child as an individual with a unique pattern of growth and development that should be nurtured.[12]

In some areas of the United States, community colleges are offering two-year programs that allow students interested in child-care careers to earn an associate of arts degree in early childhood development. College officials believe the programs will help increase the supply of quality teachers and aides, which in turn could prompt higher pay for caregivers. One innovative program began early in 1990 in Montgomery County, Maryland. In cooperation with a local college, county officials set up a service corps to provide workers for community day-care centers, nursing homes, and facilities for the disabled. The young people who remain in the corps for two years can receive vouchers or grants up to $5,000 to pay for housing and classes at the college. Corps members also are paid an hourly wage by the facilities that hire them for intern jobs.

Yet as administrators of child-care facilities across the country try to increase and improve the quality of staff and raise wages, they usually must charge parents higher rates, which can be a hardship on families already having a difficult time paying for child care. The average annual cost for a preschooler is between $3,000 and $5,000, and the cost of infant care can be much higher. For most low-income families, child care consumes about 25 percent of earnings.

Federal grants to states, provided by recent child-care legislation, can help some low-income families pay child-care costs. But some states—notably California, Massachusetts, Minnesota, and New York—already are using their tax funds not only to help subsidize day-care fees but also to increase salaries of day-care providers.

Local governments have initiated programs to help with staffing problems and to regulate and hopefully to improve the overall quality of day care, whether in centers or private homes. One example is Madison, Wisconsin. The city provides assistance for low-income families who use centers and family day-care homes certified by the city's Day Care Unit. Madison also offers grants to train child-care providers and to buy major equipment or upgrade child-care facilities.

As communities try to find ways to develop quality child-care facilities, many have set up task forces to identify the types of child care needed. In some cities, a child-care coordinator may be hired to act as a liaison between those trying to develop day-care facilities and local or state regulatory officials. A coordinator can explain zoning requirements, standards, or other regulations that must be met.

4

"Family-Friendly" Companies

From the outside, the building looks like an ordinary factory with a typical California facade of peach-colored stucco. It sits along the railroad track and near a fenced drainage trough that spills into the Pacific Ocean a couple of blocks away. At the rear of the main building, a small sign on a gate announces the "Great Pacific Child Development Center."

Once on the other side of the gate, the scene changes dramatically. A maze of tree-shaded walkways leads through outdoor play areas designed for children ranging from toddlers to school age. From the play areas, doors open into separate pods or classrooms, a nursery, and a cafeteria. All of the complex is part of a Ventura, California, day-care facility connected to the Lost Arrow Corporation. The company makes mountain-climbing gear and outdoor clothing carrying the Patagonia label.

Since it is lunchtime, a dozen or so Lost Arrow employees are in the cafeteria, some at tables eating with their children who are enrolled

A mother drops in at the on-site day-care center to visit with her son and to help feed him lunch.

in the day-care center. Several parents have gone into one of the classroom areas to visit with their preschoolers. One mom is in the nursery, making herself comfortable in a rocker before nursing her infant son. A father in the toddler play area is watching his daughter who has just asked him to count "one-two-three-go" so she and her friend can have a tricycle "race." In another part of the complex, a group of youngsters is returning from a field trip—they've been for a ride in specially built wagons that carry six toddlers, three to a side, and can be pulled to nearby stores, the beach, the post office, or other place of interest.

The Greater Pacific Child Development Center is part of what Malinda and Yvon Chouinard, the owners of Lost Arrow, call "a family affair." The Chouinards began the center in 1984 because they had two children of their own, and Malinda especially knew the conflicts that child-care problems can create for working women. Since 60 percent of the 265 employees at Lost Arrow are women, the need for an on-site day-care center seemed obvious to the Chouinards. Although there is a tuition fee for each child, the company pays 40 percent of the cost.

Lost Arrow operates under a policy that says that child care is not just an employee problem but "a problem belonging to everyone." Thus, the work environment is integrated with a child-centered environment. As a company brochure states: "Parents have the opportunity to merge their 'working self' with their 'parenting self.' Therefore, much anxiety and frustration in children and their parents is minimized."

Why Companies Help With Day Care

The Lost Arrow philosophy is one that other U.S. companies and businesses as well as government agencies have been proclaiming recently, not only in words but also in deeds. Why are companies providing help with child care? The reasons are varied, but primarily employers have discovered child care is good for business.

A scene from the play area of the on-site day-care center connected with the Lost Arrow Corporation in Ventura, California.

In the first place, many businesses have become painfully aware of the declining labor force, which is growing by only 1 percent annually compared to over 2 percent a year in previous decades. Since the supply of workers is expected to dwindle through the 1990s, employers want incentives that will attract workers and keep them. Thus many employers are beginning to take note of family needs.

For example, in families with both parents working outside the home, fathers may be responsible for part-time child care. Such fathers may refuse to take jobs that require long periods away from home or major disruptions in family life. In other instances, mothers may be offered promotions to executive positions but opt to take lesser jobs, or even part-time work, in order to have more time with their families. These types of choices can affect the productivity and growth of a company. In fact, a *Fortune* magazine survey found that when employees were concerned about child-care problems, their productivity was likely to suffer, and they would be more likely to take time off the job.

Several studies by government agencies, child development consultants, and business experts have shown that "family-friendly" corporations, those offering child-care services, attract qualified and dedicated employees. With on-site day care, there is less employee tardiness and absenteeism. Parents do not have to rush to a child-care provider far from work or miss work because child care is not available.

When parents are at ease about their children's care, morale improves, stress levels drop, and employees want to stay with a company. A divorced father with custody of three children put it this way:

> Before our company provided on-site day care, I had to take one child to a baby-sitter in the neighborhood, another to a day-care center, and the third to a school program that provides care for kids before classes begin. After work I'd have to rush to all three places to pick up the kids. It was a real hassle. Now I can be more

relaxed on my job, knowing the kids are okay and that they'll all
be in a safe place until I can take them home. [1]

One major corporation found that by initiating a child-care
program only 2 percent of the women who had taken maternity leaves
quit their jobs. Before the program began, 25 percent quit. A survey
by Du Pont of its 100,000 employees found that half of the women
and one-fourth of the men who responded had considered leaving the
company to work for a firm that balanced family and work needs. In
another study, a national insurance firm concluded that the
productivity lost when an employee quits and finding and training a
new employee can cost almost as much as the first-year salary for the
new recruit.

Anita Garaway-Furtaw, director of Lost Arrow's child-care
center, explained that her company found "supporting an on-site
child-care program is a truly cost-effective mechanism." The company
has saved about $120,000 a year. Some of the savings come from state
tax deductions that employers may claim for establishing child-care
programs. There also has been a decline in retraining costs. Owner
Yvon Chouinard said that day care "keeps five to ten people a year
from having to quit, which saves us a lot of money."

The day-care program at Lost Arrow has been able to reduce stress
also. Garaway-Furtaw pointed out that just going into the nursery and
rocking and cuddling a baby "has a soothing effect on people. Having
children around also softens the workplace. The presence of children
on the work site makes a statement that the employer genuinely cares
about its employees." Summing it up, she noted: "For everything we
have spent in terms of our ongoing subsidy, we have saved. It works
for the kids, it works for the parents, and it works for the company,
and we're not spending any money on it." [2]

The Union Bank in Monterey Park, California, has reported
similar savings because of on-the-job day care. Employees using
on-site day care were absent an average of 4.6 days compared to
nonusers who average 6.3 days. More than 70 percent of those who

applied for work at the bank said they did so because of the day-care program.

In Corvallis, Oregon, a day-care center within the Heart of the Valley Nursing Home has helped the nursing home cut not only employee absenteeism but also turnover of workers. Because 93 percent of the employees at the nursing home are women and more than 40 percent are single mothers with preschool children, there is a definite need for child care. Employees pay part of the child-care costs, and the nursing home underwrites the rest. The center is also open to the public, and parents pay full fees for child care.

Although operating expenses for the day-care center at the Corvallis nursing home totaled more than the income for the first two years, the center now breaks even. In addition, the turnover rate among employees who use the day-care center is significantly lower than among other staff members who do not use or need the center services. By retaining employees, the nursing home can save about $35,000 per year in costs to train new workers. Some employees have turned down better-paying jobs because of the child-care benefits they receive at the nursing home.

Who Cares?

Classified advertising in metropolitan newspapers clearly shows that offering child-care benefits to employees is a selling point for companies trying to recruit new workers. This trend began slowly in the 1960s and 1970s with a few major corporations offering on-site day care or child care at nearby centers at costs for employees' children well below "market rates." Now over 5,000 companies have become involved in a variety of child-care services, although that number is still a small portion of the six million or more businesses in the nation.

One major company, Marriott Corporation, recently opened a new on-site day-care center at its headquarters in Bethesda, Maryland. According to a *Washington Post* report, the center not only will provide care for employees' children but will also be a model for a service that the company hopes to sell to other businesses, universities, and hospitals. Marriott owns part interest in Corporate Child Care, a national company that sets up and operates child-care services for corporations. Marriott and Corporate Child Care executives say they expect to see such services expand greatly in the years ahead.[3]

In some communities, developers of office centers and malls build child-care facilities as incentives for tenants and their workers. The new three-story Crescent office building in northern New Jersey, for example, includes a spacious child-care center and play area. Local governments in many California communities require that builders include child-care facilities among the homes, condominiums, or apartments that they build in large housing complexes. In Sacramento, California, developers are planning a suburban community with a variety of housing surrounding a village green that includes offices, retail shops, a library, a playground, and a day-care center.

The U.S. Defense Department provides subsidized day-care facilities for thousands of children whose parents are in the armed forces and live on military bases in the United States and other countries. Federal legislation requires that space be provided free for on-site day care in any federal building. For example, space has been provided in the Senate Office Building for the Senate Employees Child Center, and the Central Intelligence Agency (CIA) has provided space for its Children's Center in Langley, Virginia, which opened in the fall of 1989.

Usually on-site or near-site centers are open from 6:30 or 7:00 A.M. to 6:30 or 7:00 P.M. But many companies work several shifts. In fact, at least 16 percent of U.S. workers are on the job in the evening, late at night, or early in the morning. Thus employees need care for their children at varied hours. For example, Chrysler Corporation employees at a plant in Huntsville, Alabama, can place their children in an on-site facility that is open twenty hours a day. In Ocala, Florida, Certified Grocers opened an on-site child-care center primarily to serve employees who work non-daytime shifts; parents could find only child-care providers who operated during traditional working hours.

46

In Mishawaka, Indiana, Nyloncraft, a subsidiary of Excel Industries, provides twenty-four-hour service at its Learning Center for employees' children. The Mishawaka center transports children to and from school and also takes some children to a company plant in neighboring South Bend, delivering youngsters to their parents after they have finished working the late shift.

Another twenty-four-hour care facility is the Little Eagles Child Care Center at the Syracuse Regional Postal Center in New York, which cares for children eight weeks old and up. The center was designed to accommodate parents who work either the day or night shift. As an administrator at the center put it: "The twenty-four-hour day care is an incentive I use when hiring people. They're willing to work odd hours because of the child care."

A rather unusual day-care center to accommodate the unpredictable hours of construction workers has been set up by the

After picking up her two youngsters from an on-site day-care center in the federal building where she works, this Portland (Oregon) mother heads for home.

B. E. & K. Corporation based in Birmingham, Alabama. The company builds industrial facilities and recently worked on the expansion of a papermaking plant near Savannah, Georgia. Since 11 percent of the construction company's work force of 600 or more were local women and valued carpenters, electricians, welders, and other skilled employees, the company had to find ways to keep them on the job. Most of the women have children who need care, but nearby child-care facilities were full or closed at times when construction work had to be done.

B. E. & K. decided to set up its own center near the construction site, using five forty-foot mobile homes that can be expanded if needed. When the construction project was completed in Georgia, the company was able to move the mobile day-care center to the next site. Some of the workers moved with the company because of the flexible day-care available.[4]

Hospitals are prime examples of employers who offer on-site day care around the clock. In 1984, the Rapides General Hospital in Alexandria, Louisiana, constructed a model $350,000 child-care facility across the street from the hospital. Parents can monitor their children's activities via a closed-circuit television hookup or can visit when they wish. It is no secret that the center improves staff recruitment. As a Rapides hospital vice president explained: "Let's face it. The competition is tough for a good RN or pharmacy employee, and they're not flocking to this area in droves." The center provides a needed service for workers and also benefits the hospital and patients because employees give full attention to their jobs.

On-site day care may not always mean placing a child in a center. Some employers allow a parent to bring a child into the office or other workplace. A librarian in Pennsylvania, for example, took her infant son to the library with her. While Mom worked, the baby slept in a portable crib or was carried in a baby pack as Mom went about her routine tasks. In other instances, company executives—both mothers and fathers—have taken children to the office with them. The children sleep or play while the parents work at their desks.

It's part of the daily routine for many parents—dropping children off at a day-care center—before going to their jobs. This mother feels that a quality center helps her child develop educationally and emotionally.

A few lawyers, teachers at preschools, commercial artists, editors, accountants, and other professionals have taken their infants along to work also. In one unusual situation, a taxi driver in Washington, D.C., took her infant daughter along during the workday, strapping the baby into a car seat for the ride, not a recommended form of child care but one the woman felt fit her needs at the time.

Joint Efforts

Some employers, of course, feel that supporting an on-site day-care facility is not practical. For one thing, large companies may have plants or retail operations in many different locations in a region or across the nation. Opening an on-site day-care center at each location could be very expensive since setting up just one new center can cost hundreds of thousands of dollars (estimates have ranged from $200,000 to well over $500,000 for construction of a center, depending on size and location).

In some instances, branches of large companies and smaller firms are pooling their resources to set up facilities that serve the day-care needs of their combined employees. Some examples:

—In Atlanta, Georgia, the Downtown Child Development Center is located inside a major department store. It provides day care not only for children of store employees but also for children of employees in five downtown firms.

—In West Los Angeles, California, Capital Cities/ABC, Inc., Act III Communications, Creative Artists Agency, and Home Box Office, Inc., joined forces to fund a $3 million child-care center that serves eighty children.

—In the Washington, D.C. area, several businesses share the costs of the Tysons Play and Learn Center at Tysons Corner. Companies reserve spaces for their employees' children, and demand has been so great that the center had to expand its facilities after only three years of operation. It now accommodates 164 children.

Another type of arrangement was initiated several years ago by Cray Research, a computer company in Chippewa Falls, Wisconsin, a small community with only a few day-care facilities. Cray, which employs a large number of professional workers, knew that offering child-care benefits would help them attract and retain employees. The company decided to work with the local YMCA, which wanted to develop a day-care program for the entire community. However, the YMCA could not afford the costs for the facility without passing those costs on to families, many of whom would not be able to pay high day-care fees.

As a result, Cray set up a matching program. According to a report in *Management Accounting,* "Cray and its employees donated funds to construct a day care facility to accommodate 150 children. The facility is owned and operated by the YMCA, which now . . . can provide economical day care to the entire community." However, spaces are reserved for children of Cray employees.[5]

Other Initiatives

For some family-friendly companies, on-site or nearby day-care facilities are not the most appropriate child-care service to offer employees. After first surveying their employees, some companies have found that employees need or want other types of child-care services, which include a variety of options.

Assistance with child-care costs is one kind of benefit. In some cases, this may be a plan approved by the Internal Revenue Service that allows employers to pay workers' child-care costs from pretax earnings. In other words, workers pay for the child care, but they do not have to pay federal taxes on the amount used for that purpose.

Some companies offer employees vouchers or grants to pay a portion of a child-care bill. A chain of forty-one Burger King restaurants in northern Indiana and southern Michigan, for example, pays workers up to $45 per week as a child-care allowance. It was one way that the company could recruit and retain employees.

As increasing number of companies are offering workers the services of child-care resource and referral (R & R) centers. Such centers compile information about child-care facilities, usually on a computer data base, and are common in most metropolitan areas and at many universities. Employers pay the costs of R & R. For example, Mobil Oil Corporation near Washington, D.C., has invested about $85,000 in a referral service that helps employees find quality child care. In addition, Giant Food and Potomac Electric located in the area also are providing R & R benefits for their employees.

Along with offering R & R services, some employers may provide vouchers or grants to subsidize child-care costs, but primarily an employer provides referral services to cut down on the time workers must be off the job to search for quality child care. Resource centers help parents determine what kind(s) of care the family needs, what suitable programs are available to them at affordable fees, and what facilities are licensed or are not required to be licensed.

In some instances, a R & R service may include a network of nearby family day-care homes that employees can use. Steelcase of Grand Rapids, Michigan, set up such a network and also hired a child-care coordinator who visits the homes to insure that they meet quality standards. Another example is Lincoln National Corporation, an insurance firm in Fort Wayne, Indiana, which also monitors family day-care providers serving its employees. In addition, the company offers caregivers information that will help them provide more professional services.

As family demands encroach on the workplace, a growing number of companies are allowing nontraditional work schedules, usually called "flextime." With flextime, employees may set up work schedules to fit family routines or, perhaps, vary their work hours on a daily basis. According to the *Harvard Business Review,* "flextime is now used by about 12% of all U.S. workers, while half the country's large employers offer some kind of flextime arrangement." [6]

Flextime arrangements include working part time when an employee needs to provide extended care for a child or other dependent family member. Some employees work longer days (ten hours usually) and a four-day week. Others are involved in job-sharing arrangements—for example, two people work the same job but split the hours between them.

Another type of flextime arrangement is to work at home, using computers and modems to connect with office terminals. Home-based work is becoming an increasingly attractive alternative in southern California since the region's Air Quality Board has ruled that employers in the metropolitan areas may be fined if they do not cut back on the number of employees who commute. Heavy traffic is clogging the highways and contributing to some of the worst air pollution in the nation.

Parental leave to care for family members is still one more kind of flexibility. Whether or not state laws require such leaves, some companies offer these benefits. About 40 percent of full-time workers in large- or medium-size American companies are allowed to take unpaid maternity or paternity leave up to twenty weeks. Some major firms such as IBM allow up to three years unpaid leave; employees are guaranteed not only their jobs on return but also are able to maintain their health insurance and retirement benefits while on leave.

Recent reports indicate that more fathers are taking advantage of parental leave plans. A few major companies say that since they initiated family leave plans in the late 1980s, the number of men interested in or actually taking time off to care for newborns has doubled or tripled. Yet there are many men who still hesitate to take paternity leave, even when offered, because they feel that child care is a "woman's job" or feel the pressure of others who conform to stereotyped rules for men and women.

5

School Programs

Schools for the Twenty-First Century.

Schools in banks and airports.

Schools as "drop-off" centers.

Schools that seldom close.

Schools for teenage mothers.

Across the nation, diverse types of schools are the settings not only for educational programs but also for child-care services. Linking schools and child care has been one thrust of preschool programs for many years and now is emphasized in a variety of before- and after-school programs for older children and in-school programs for teenage parents.

Preschools

"If someone gave me a multibillion-dollar gift and asked me to spend it on a single program that would do most for young Americans, I'd put it into a universal system of day-care centers, nursery schools, and kindergartens," wrote Harold Howe, II, an education professor at Harvard and author of several books and many articles on education.

Howe believes that early childhood education helps improve a child's social, physical, and intellectual development and thus his or her chances for succeeding in later schooling and life experiences.[1]

Some preschool programs are part of private day nurseries supported by parents who are able to pay fairly high fees to provide activities that give their children an "edge" or running start in life. But a variety of preschool programs are government-funded or supported by foundations or civic or religious groups.

One nonprofit preschool program in a Chicago suburb is being conducted at Oak Forest High School. Twelve preschoolers are enrolled, and that same number of teenagers work with the youngsters under the supervision of adult teachers. The program is part of a child-care class at the high school and has been designed to help

Reading to children is an important part of the daily routine in many day-care and preschool facilities across the nation.

teenagers who want to learn about early childhood development or who just like to work with children.

How does the program work? During part of the class, a teacher conducts a learning session with the preschoolers while teenagers watch and listen. The preschoolers may name the days of the week or identify colors of animals or discuss community workers like firefighters and police officers. Later, teenagers work with youngsters on a one-to-one basis, helping them color, cut, or paste. The teenagers also take part in play activities with the youngsters—one child may need help building a tower with blocks; another may need help winding up a toy; still another youngster may need instructions on how to work a simple puzzle. Sometimes the teenagers help youngsters learn to share or to be polite and use such terms as "please," "thank you," and "excuse me."

Yet the preschoolers also teach the teenagers. Some of the teenagers have learned patience, responsibility, and child-care skills that they have been able to apply within their own families or will apply when they have children of their own.

Getting a Head Start

Unlike the Oak Forest preschool, most programs that serve preschoolers are separate entities, sometimes located in buildings of their own. They may be known by any one of a number of titles, such as Head Start, Prekindergarten Programs for At Risk Children, or developmental preschools. Head Start is the most widely publicized and one of the most successful preschool programs.

Many Head Start programs began during the 1960s as part of President Lyndon Johnson's War on Poverty. They have provided a way to help needy three- to five-year-olds prepare for elementary school. Preschool play activities in Head Start and similar programs are designed to help children learn how to analyze, to work independently, and also to develop social skills—learn how to get along with others. In addition, the programs provide nutritious meals, inoculations for childhood diseases, and medical and dental exams.

Involving parents in their children's learning is one of the major strengths of the Head Start programs. Parents are encouraged to read to their children, to get involved as aides in the classroom, and to help make decisions regarding their children's education. Parental involvement shows youngsters that school is important and encourages children to strive for success. It also motivates parents to go on with their own schooling and to prepare for a career or learn skills for advancement on a job.

A Michigan educational foundation conducted a long-term study of poor children who had been in Ypsilanti's Perry Preschool programs between 1962 and 1967. Researchers tracked the students' progress until they were nineteen years old and found that youngsters develop "a firmer foundation on which to mature and prosper." Students in the preschool programs were more likely to be employed or in college than those from low-income families who were not involved in early-learning programs. Children who receive little or no help in early learning tend to fall behind in class activities. If that becomes a pattern, children may feel they cannot succeed and drop out of school, thus limiting their opportunities for employment and other types of achievements.

Because the Michigan students who had been in preschool programs were not likely to be dropouts, welfare recipients, or participants in crime, the study concluded that the investment in early learning saved at least three dollars for every dollar spent. A more recent study by the National Committee for Economic Development, a group of prominent business and education leaders, found that every dollar spent on quality preschool education saves up to six dollars in later government costs for remedial education, welfare, crime protection, and similar social services.

Business and education leaders along with government officials have been calling for expansion of the Head Start programs, and several hundred million dollars in additional funds already have been earmarked for that purpose. The goal is to reach 2.5 million youngsters between three and five years old. As a *Fortune* magazine report pointed out:

> Study after study demonstrates that Head Start by and large does what it was designed to do. The program is *not* an all-purpose antitoxin for the multiple afflictions of modern-day poverty. But it does enable most participants to enter kindergarten better prepared intellectually, emotionally, and socially than their non-preschool peers.[2]

Yet many children who are at risk do not receive help in their early years. In Illinois, for example, Voices for Illinois Children, an advocacy group of business and civic leaders, estimates that 127,000 children in the state need early-learning programs but only about one-third of that number are getting help. Voices has urged the state of Illinois to provide more grants so that local schools can set up preschool programs. The group suggested that the Chicago school board use its preschool funds to contract with nonprofit groups to provide preschool programs, especially in neighborhoods where schools are crowded and classrooms are not available.

Voices also recommended that day-care centers include early-learning activities. According to the advocacy group, many Chicago day-care centers, like those in other cities, are understaffed, and most caregivers are poorly trained. Thus children get little mental stimulation, which can help prepare them for formal schooling. As a *Chicago Tribune* editorial noted: "It is inexcusable to warehouse children in 'day-care slots' without providing stimulating opportunities to learn."[3]

Getting prepared for elementary school is of course what kindergartens have been about for many years. Most states do not require kindergarten classes, but school districts that offer kindergarten usually have half-day sessions. However, in many parts of the nation, kindergarten is being expanded to six hours, a regular school day. The trend has been prompted by studies that show all-day kindergarten provides better preparation for first grade and improves students' scores on standardized tests. In addition, all-day kindergarten benefits working parents whose children need care during the day.

However, critics of expanded kindergarten argue that five-year-olds have a short attention span and that being in a formal school setting all day could be stressful. Some experts in early childhood development also oppose combining day care with formal schooling—they believe day care should be like an extension of the family. They fear that teachers trained in elementary education would put too much pressure on learning academic skills and rigid discipline, which could prove harmful to young children.

A few psychologists have contended that children get "burned out"—tired of school—if they start too early. Some suggest that formal learning should not even begin until about seven or eight years old and that children should be taught informally at home until that time. But, as has been stated previously, millions of parents must work outside the home and are unable to provide the kinds of activities that prepare children for schooling.

Twenty-first Century Schools

The controversy over whether schools should be linked with child care will continue in the years ahead. In the meantime, several million three- and four-year-olds are enrolled in the nation's public and private nursery schools. And prekindergarten classes for four-year-olds are already being offered in the public school districts of more than thirty states.

Many educators and social service providers believe this trend will continue and that early learning and child care will be a common part of public schools in the next century. As a report in *Newsweek* noted: " . . . about 15 percent of the nation's local districts now offer some form of child care, or allow community groups to use their buildings. Many programs continue during vacations, and a few run even in the summer; some extend into junior high school." [4]

Psychology Professor Edward Zeigler, director of the Bush Center in Child Development at Yale University, is one person who has long advocated using schools not only for formal education but also as day-care and family-resource centers. Developer of the Head Start program that was designed to involve parents and the community, Zeigler has been called the architect for a model "Twenty-first Century School." Basically, he recommends using public school buildings for more than formal schooling, providing social services for families, including care for preschoolers and school-age children before and after school hours.

The first Twenty-first Century School program was implemented in 1988 in two Missouri school districts made up primarily of middle- to upper-middle-income families. Several programs also are under way in other states, including Connecticut, Colorado, Wyoming, Wisconsin, and Ohio.

In Connecticut, a pilot project using Zeigler's model is part of the Betances School in downtown Hartford. The principal, Edna Negron, explained to a *New York Times* reporter that because of poverty many children in the neighborhood must overcome barriers to learning. "Physical exercise, the development of large and small motor skills, is important for reading and writing," Negron said. "But we have had fifth and sixth graders who couldn't jump rope, and . . . couldn't run and kick at the same time." She also pointed out that "families don't talk to their children. We have kids who arrive at kindergarten unable to put together a sentence." [5]

Open thirteen hours a day, the Betances School is now more like a community center, offering day care for young children and care for school-age children. There is a summer program for children and a Family Resource Center that trains women in the neighborhood who will provide family day care in their homes. Family counseling and a program to prevent teenage pregnancy are part of the project as well.

Before- and After-School Programs

Not all schools can be adapted for such comprehensive programs as the Twenty-first Century idea. Many schools in urban areas are overcrowded, and there are not enough funds to pay for the support services that families need. Lack of transportation to and from the school may also be a problem. But a growing number of schools have been able to provide before- and after-school programs. By the most recent estimate, 25 percent of the nation's schools have such programs for latchkey kids.

Some of the programs are organized and paid for by parents, and the school provides space, including use of a gymnasium and/or all-purpose room, or perhaps a portable classroom placed on the playground. Other programs may be initiated by teachers or principals who see the need. Wellesley College in Massachusetts has developed the School-Age Child Care Project that provides information on school-based care. So does the National Association for the Education of Young Children.

In one southern California school district, more than 12 percent of the 9,000 youngsters from kindergarten through fifth grade are in school-based child care. Parents pay monthly fees to cover the costs of renting space in school buildings, janitorial services, and business expenses. In some cases, grants from the state help pay fees for low-income families.

In some communities, school officials, civic groups, and local government agencies work together to initiate before- and after-school programs. An after-school program in a northern Indiana town began as a cooperative effort that included support of the Youth Coalition Project (an on-going program for youth), the privately funded Youth Services Bureau, the school system, and the county park department. Students in grades four through eight are involved, taking part in tutoring programs, field trips, drama, music, art, sports, and games.

A school-based program called CAP (Children at Play) in Arlington Heights, Illinois, is operated by the park district and serves seven

Above: Young people getting a look at a freight yard in Oxnard, California. *Below:* Children from a day-care center listen to an art museum curator explain about collections of paintings and sculpture on display. Field trips provide educational opportunities that might not be available otherwise to some children.

elementary schools, which provide space for activities. At one school, between twenty-five and thirty children from kindergarten through fifth grade take part under the supervision of Jeanne Smith, who calls herself a "substitute mom," and two aides. Smith and her aides prepare snacks for the children, supervise outdoor play or indoor games, encourage students to complete homework assignments, or work with them on craft projects.

However, Smith believes one of the most important parts of the CAP program is giving kids attention, praise, and affection. As she put it, she tries to give the children "everything I want my own children to have coming home from school." [6]

Directors of school-age child care frequently say that programs should be structured but activities should be as relaxed as possible—more like being at home than in school. Many stress that learning often goes on in school-based child care, but the learning does not necessarily come from books. Games and activities often help youngsters learn by doing; they develop creativity and social skills. They may also learn about resources in their own communities or neighborhoods, especially if field trips to local parks, museums, and other facilities are part of the programs.

Many school-age child-care programs are conducted in facilities away from school. Religious groups, civic organizations and clubs, social service agencies, and park departments may provide such services. During the summer, at least five million school-age children attend day camps or day programs that offer care and supervision along with a variety of activities.

Some summer camps are extensions of after-school programs, while others serve the emotionally and physically disabled or are organized around particular interests, such as music or sports. A full summer resident program of academics and recreation costing several thousand dollars is the type of camp that usually only the affluent can afford.

In some instances, after-school programs are designed to use inner-city adolescents between the ages of ten and fifteen as helpers

Many after-school and summer programs for so-called "latchkey kids" include sports activities. Here Shawn Kemp, (standing, right) forward with the Seattle SuperSonics, talks with young people involved in Kemp's basketball clinic held in his home town of Elkhart, Indiana.

in day-care centers for younger children. Called Early Adolescent Helper Programs, they began through the efforts of the National Commission on Resources for Youth to promote youth participation in community agencies. Most of the young people involved have been high school students, but an increasing number of children from sixth grade up have become helpers. They act as aides in preschools, day-care centers, and latchkey programs, helping out with activities that range from block-building to storytelling to being escorts on field trips. They also help out at senior centers.

A report in *Children Today* explained that the Helper Programs not only provide extra hands in child-care facilities but also motivate young people to stay in school and to learn about the work world. "Moreover, [the program] bolsters self-esteem . . . as the Helpers find themselves entrusted with real responsibilities and as they receive recognition and appreciation for their participation." Young people themselves say that they gain as much from the program as they give. As one helper reportedly put it, "Some people need you as much as you need them to talk over things or problems." [7]

Workplace Schools

A fairly recent innovation is the workplace school, which is much more than day care for employees' children. Often called a satellite school, it provides regular schooling along with day care and is a cooperative effort between business firms and school districts. Usually, businesses provide free space and perhaps the cost of utilities and maintenance, while the school district supplies staff and educational materials. Parents pay the fees for the day care after school hours.

Employers invest in the program because, as with on-the-job day care, the costs are recovered through reduced absenteeism and higher productivity of employees. School districts like the idea because it helps reduce overcrowding in some schools and often saves on transportation costs since parents take their children along to work and drop them off at the schools. Another advantage, parents say, is that they are more involved in their children's care and learning experiences, and youngsters are more secure knowing their parents are nearby.

Although some educators and political leaders have criticized the concept, suggesting that the workplace schools will be for the elite, others say that the satellite schools provide better cultural and economic integration than some suburban or inner-city schools. As one administrator explained, children of company executives are enrolled right along with the children of clerks and janitors.

In Florida, about a dozen satellite schools are open or in the planning stages. One has been operating successfully since 1987 at the Miami International Airport, where the school serves employees' children from kindergarten through second grade. Other workplace schools in the Miami metropolitan and suburban areas have been set up at such diverse sites as an insurance company, hospital, community college, and government office building.

The Miami workplace school idea has been the model for a similar effort in Minnesota. The St. Paul First Bank System and the school district have set up a program in the downtown facilities of the bank. Bank employees with children ages four through six can enroll their youngsters in the combination school (kindergarten and first grade) and day care. Corporations in New York City and other major metropolitan areas around the country are also studying the possibility of workplace schools.

Day Care for Children of Teen Parents

A century ago, it was common for young people in their late teen years to finish their schooling, start working in a chosen occupation, marry, and begin having their families. By the end of World War II, an increasing number of teenagers were staying in school longer—taking college courses or getting degrees in higher education—and waiting until their early twenties before establishing a career and family life. Over the past few decades, the situation has changed. Although the birth *rate* for teenage parents has not increased, there are a greater number of girls age fifteen and under having babies.

Adolescent parents have become a major national concern since teen parents are more inclined to have social and economic problems than many young people who delay parenthood until their mid-twenties. Many teen mothers are single and poor. They also are apt to give birth to underweight (under five pounds eight ounces) babies, who are "forty times more likely to die in the first month of life than those weighing more," according to a report in *Children Today*. Many low-birthweight babies suffer from such long-term disabilities as chronic lung diseases, mental retardation, blindness, and cerebral palsy. Lifetime health care for low-birthweight babies and lost earnings because of disabilities cost the nation billions of dollars. Yet prenatal care to prevent the conditions that lead to such disabilities or programs to prevent adolescent pregnancies cost only a few hundred dollars per teenager.[8]

Another major concern is the fact that teenage parents are likely to be unemployed or working at jobs that pay only the minimum wage. Many pregnant teenagers drop out of school, which could mean living in poverty for a lifetime. About half of the 500,000 teenagers who give birth to children each year are under the age of eighteen and never complete high school. But in a dozen or so states, some programs are being set up to help teen mothers stay in school. Most of the programs include some kind of day care for children.

Just a few decades ago, the question of whether to provide day care for children of parents still in high school or even college was hardly a matter of serious discussion. Pregnant teenagers usually were expelled from high school and not encouraged to continue schooling after their children were born. Today, however, child care is important not only because it helps young parents complete their formal education but also because programs for teenage parents usually include classes in parenting skills and in child development. Frequently, teenagers in the programs have come from abusive homes, and their parents may have put them out because of their pregnancies.

Seldom are fathers around to help the new mothers who see their babies as the only source of love, someone they can hang on to.

New Futures School in Albuquerque, New Mexico, is a model for educational and political leaders in other states who are trying to keep teenage parents in school. New Futures, which began as a volunteer effort in the YWCA, has been operating for more than twenty years. Child care, counseling, health services, and job placement after graduation are all part of the program.

A similar program has been in place since the early 1980s at the Rindge and Latin School in Cambridge, Massachusetts, the only public high school in the city. Called the Adolescent Parenting Program, it provides care for the children of teenage parents in the First Steps center located on the first floor of the school.

Several high schools in Georgia offer on-site day care for children of teenage parents, but in Atlanta, a First Step Family Support Project in Carver High School is as comprehensive as the New Futures School and the Cambridge program. The Georgia Department of Human Resources and the Atlanta school system sponsor the First Step Project, which is limited to twenty high school girls, although any Carver student who has a child can use the day care center. Like parenting programs in other states, the Carver First Step Project offers child care development classes, counseling, and tutorial aid, all designed to keep girls in school until they graduate. In addition, the First Step Project helps teenage mothers get part time work and places them in government-funded housing.

What is the day like for a teenage mother in this type of parenting program? It starts early, perhaps just at dawn when mother and child must get out of bed and get ready to go to the bus stop for the ride to school. When a young mom (call her Ann) arrives at the school about an hour before classes begin, she helps her son from the bus, juggles books and tote bag, and heads for the day-care center. There Ann meets and gossips with other teenage moms, makes sure her son gets settled, talks for a few minutes with the coordinator of the program, then goes to the school cafeteria for breakfast.

Once the first bell rings, Ann blends into the usual high school routine. After lunch break, she visits her son in the day-care center, then heads for her part-time job at a nearby office, where she works as a clerical aide. It is nearly 5:00 P.M. when she picks up her son to ride the bus home. But the day is hardly over. There is dinner to cook, a child to bathe and read to, and the inevitable homework and load of laundry to do.

Although parenting programs are not easy for teenage mothers, who frequently say they never realized how much work and responsibility are involved in caring for children, the programs have successfully kept girls in school. Most graduates are placed in jobs or go on to college.

In recent years, educators also have begun to recognize the need for day care at the college level, helping young parents, who are students, continue their education. In some instances, a university may operate a center on campus and hire students as staff. Other schools provide space and maintenance but contract with independent chains to staff and operate the centers. Kinder-Care, for example, is responsible for operations at a new day-care center on the Newark campus of the University of Medicine and Dentistry of New Jersey. Up to 165 children from six weeks to twelve years old can be accommodated.

However, day-care centers on college campuses usually are rare and, when available, have long lists of children waiting to be enrolled or are too expensive for low-income students. The lack of affordable day care on campus is one of the major barriers to higher education for students whose families are poor, according to the Children's Defense Fund. Only a few states such as New York, Minnesota, and California subsidize child care for parents who are college students.

6
___

Special Kinds of Care

Brandon gets the flu. Heather comes down with a severe cold. Cecil gets chicken pox. Brandon, Heather, and Cecil are all under five years old and usually go to a day-care center while their parents are on the job. But a child with a contagious illness usually is not welcome in a day-care center or family day-care home. What do parents do?

In most cases, parents must take time off from their jobs to stay with sick children or find caregivers who will come into their home. But in recent years, some special facilities, such as a day-care service called Tender Care for Kids in Minneapolis, Minnesota, have been set up to care for sick children. Tender Care provides nursing services for children at home, in an isolation section of a day-care center, and in a special section of a hospital sometimes called a sick bay.

Another group of children who need special day care are the disabled, youngsters with physical and/or mental handicaps, and those who test positive for the HIV virus, which sometimes leads to acquired immune deficiency syndrome (AIDS). Children who have been abused—emotionally, physically, or sexually—need special day-care services. So do homeless children—those whose families are literally left out in the cold.

Caring for Sick Kids

Until recent years, most employers offered little sympathy and seldom any benefits when workers had to take time away from their jobs to be at home with sick children. Employees lost wages and were expected to keep their family problems at home. Now, however, some companies provide for emergency leaves or allow employees to use sick leave or personal days to be home with their sick children (or to care for other dependent family members).

Other firms have set up cooperative programs with facilities that care for sick children for a small fee or at no cost to employees. Du Pont, a major chemical manufacturer, funds a center called Sniffles and Sneezes for employees' children in Wilmington, Delaware. The company also has made similar arrangements for sick child care in hospitals near other Du Pont plants around the country.

Government agencies also support such facilities. One example is the Hickory Dickory Doc day-care center that serves mildly sick children of county workers in Ventura County, California.

Hospitals are in the forefront when it comes to providing on-site day care for employee's children, and they also are leading the way in care for mildly ill children in special sick bays or centers. One such center, Le Joie d'Aimer (The Joy of Caring) in Philadelphia, was initiated by a nurse at the Medical College of Pennsylvania, a hospital facility that provides the space for sick children. Le Joie also cares for children whose parents must work night shifts.

Nationwide there are only about one hundred sick bays for children with minor illnesses; half of them are in pediatric wings that seldom are filled to capacity. Children with communicable diseases are separated from other pediatric patients. Most sick bays also include an all-purpose or common room where children who are well enough to be out of bed can play table games or take part in other quiet activities. Although only a few states have regulations for sick-child care programs, hospital centers usually have full-time nurses and a pediatrician on duty.

Another trend in providing care for sick children is home health services. Aides or licensed practical nurses go to a child's own home. Such a service is part of sick-child programs at hospitals. Children's Hospital in Washington, D.C., for example, has a program called Hugs and Tissues that is being promoted as a benefit that businesses can offer employees. Like other child-care programs, sick-child care can help cut down on employee absenteeism. Parent who want to use the service can preregister their children and then make the necessary arrangements when a child gets sick. Usually parents stay home with their children during the first few days of an illness, but during the recovery period the services of a home health staff person allow parents to return to their jobs.

Many health service agencies around the nation also offer such services. These agencies originally were set up to provide aides and nurses for the homebound elderly, but now send caregivers to tend to sick youngsters as well.

Care for Disabled Children

Only recently has the need for special kinds of day care for disabled children been recognized. For example, an eight-month study of child-care needs in the Philadelphia, Pennsylvania, area was completed in early 1990. The study showed that of the 60,000 disabled children about two-thirds require day care, but no suitable facilities could be found for them.

Across the United States, mothers of disabled children are among the increasing number of women entering the labor force. Like other families, those with handicapped children need the income of parents who work outside the home. Parents or other caregivers in families with disabled children (or elderly family members) also need a respite—a breather from the responsibility of constant caretaking.

Cost is a big factor in finding day care for disabled children. Many child-care centers or family day-care homes do not have provisions for wheelchairs or the special equipment needed to handle severely disabled children. Frequently, providers must hire additional staff or install special equipment. Providers usually are not trained to care for children who cannot sit upright, cannot use the toilet, or are unable to feed themselves. Caregivers also fear that they will be liable for any medical complications or accidents that might occur with handicapped children. Thus, a center or family day-care home may charge up to twice as much for care of a disabled child as for other children enrolled.

The fears and prejudices of parents whose children are able-bodied also play a part in whether disabled children will be cared for in day-care facilities. A report in the *Washington Post* described a common experience for parents of disabled children. A mother in Montgomery County, Maryland, found a family day-care home that would accept her son who has epilepsy and is mentally retarded. But according to the mother, the parents of other children enrolled protested because they didn't want their children in the same room with a boy they saw as a "freak." [1]

Another problem stems from fear of AIDS. Some parents have withdrawn their children from day-care centers that enroll youngsters infected with the HIV virus, even though infected children may not transmit the disease or show symptoms of AIDS. Health officials at the American Academy of Pediatrics, the Centers for Disease Control, and other public health agencies say that children with the HIV virus do not pose a threat to others unless they show symptoms and there is a possibility of transferring blood from one person to another (such as when children bite or have open sores).

Public health experts emphasize that AIDS is transmitted through sexual contact, contaminated needles shared by drug users, and at birth by mothers infected with AIDS. Educational campaigns have helped point up the scientific facts about the disease and have alleviated some fears. As a result, state health departments that previously barred young children with the HIV virus from day-care centers have changed their regulations. A parent and the director of Parents United for Child Care in Massachusetts explained to a *Boston Globe* reporter: "These kids [infected with the HIV virus] need as much attention as anybody else and with the proper training and facts day-care centers can handle these kids with no problem." [2]

Day Treatment Centers

Every four hours in the United States a child dies because of abuse. Hundreds of thousands more survive abuse and neglect but may require protection, hospitalization, therapy, or other services to help overcome the effects of maltreatment. One way that abused children are helped is through day treatment programs operated by public and private social service agencies.

Although a day treatment facility may look like a typical preschool or day-care center for young children, there is a big difference. Programs are designed to help children on an individual basis because of neglect or abuse. In addition, group therapy sessions help youngsters release the anger and frustration that has built up, to express themselves in healthy ways, and to overcome destructive behavior.

An essential part of any day treatment program for abused children is helping parents learn how to nurture rather than batter their children, explains Suzi Nichols, who coordinates services for a day treatment program under the auspices of the Child Abuse Prevention Services (CAPS) of Elkhart, Indiana. "One of the saddest things about abuse is that after the bruises are gone, the emotional scars remain," Nichols says. "Children who are raised in an abusive environment by parents who were abused as children will almost always 'grow up' but will suffer as adults from the lack of nurturing. Their needs not having been met, they will also be poor parents." [3]

Because it was expected of them, abusive parents expect their children to perform impossible feats, such as never reaching for a spoon while being fed or never spitting out food or never moving while being diapered or never crying when hurt. If infants or young children do not behave as expected, parents may use violent physical punishment because it is the only form of discipline they know.

Nurturing (parenting) classes at CAPS help abusive parents replace damaging child-rearing methods with healthy ways to care for their children and support their development. Classes also help parents deal with their feelings of alienation and poor self-esteem, and the hurts and devastation that come from being belittled and badgered all their lives. Volunteer parent aides work with abusive parents, developing trust and serving as models for parenting and life-management skills. Usually parent aides spend several days a week over a period of a year with parents in CAPS treatment classes.

Do programs such as CAPS work? One parent who participated in a nurturing/parenting class had been molested at the age of five by

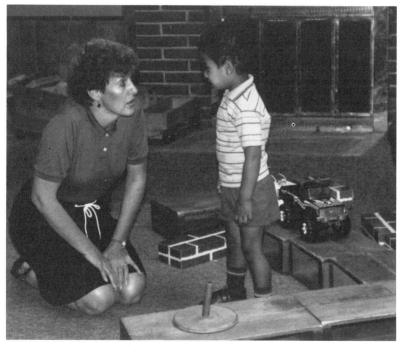

Child Abuse Prevention Services (CAPS) in Elkhart, Indiana, has set up a day treatment program for preschoolers who are victims of abuse.

a great uncle and wrote about her experiences because, as she pointed out, it was important to talk/write openly in order to be free of "self-imposed prisons of shame, guilt, and dirtiness." Another reason for writing was to help others overcome feelings that they were at fault for what happened to them as children.

> The nurturing class [at CAPS] has given me the opportunity to cry for the child in me and to allow the adult in me to love her, and nurture her.

> This class has made a big difference in my life . . . I have learned that discipline and punishment are two distinctly different methods of enforcing family rules. Coming from an abusive past, they were intertwined within my mind and were one and the same. I have learned about 'time out' both for me and for my children, and the appropriate use of 'ignoring' irritating or inappropriate behavior in my children. My children are blossoming quite well with a Mom who is no longer frustrated and angry.[4]

As more and more communities establish programs to try to prevent abuse and neglect of children, perhaps the tremendous costs for other social services and the criminal justice system can be cut. To combat the effects of violence against children, the nation spends millions of dollars each year placing abused children in foster care, providing special education and therapy, and treating those who are disabled or socially impaired because of abuse and neglect. Costs also mount as those who have suffered violent childhoods become runaways, delinquents, or adult criminals. In short, the nation spends at least ten times more treating the human and social problems that are the result of child abuse than is spent on prevention programs. As the National Committee for the Prevention of Child Abuse has stated: Most child abuse and neglect can be prevented if communities support programs to help families in stress.

Centers for Homeless Children

In some cities and towns, helping families in stress means reaching out to provide shelters for the homeless. But usually families are allowed to stay in shelters only for a limited time. Some churches, temples, or social service agencies provide overnight shelter only; homeless families must leave in the morning.

Several years ago, when Joyce Booth of Indianapolis, Indiana, became aware of the homeless in her city, she felt that her church ought to reach out to help. A number of homeless families, including women and children, were living in abandoned buildings and cars and parks. Some of the women had lost their jobs and were unable to pay for rent, food, and other basic necessities. "I learned that the women were either too proud to go to public agencies for help or did not know where to get aid," Joyce Booth says.[5]

Booth decided to take the lead in setting up a feeding program for the families and getting the church to open its doors at night so that homeless people could sleep on the pews. The next step was to build a homeless shelter on church property in downtown Indianapolis. Called Dayspring, the shelter now houses about fifty people, and children are cared for during the day while their parents look for work and a place to live.

Recognizing that parents need a safe place for their children while they are job-hunting, other groups across the nation have set up day-care centers for homeless children. The Salvation Army has been operating a drop-in day-care center for several years in downtown Cambridge, Massachusetts. Open five days a week, the center can take in only ten children per day, the maximum that state regulations allow for such facilities. However, family day-care providers in the neighborhood are trying to help out by offering a few days of care for homeless children whenever the Salvation Army facility is full.

In San Francisco, a group of social service agencies and businesses are sponsoring a center for homeless children in the city.

The center opened in late 1990 and is designed to care for fifteen children. Families stay at a city-operated shelter at night.

Another day-care center for homeless children opened in Washington, D.C., in the spring of 1990. Called Kidspace, it is located in the basement all-purpose room in the Miles Memorial Christian Methodist Episcopal Church, which provides the space free. Social service groups pay the cost of utilities and refer children to Kidspace. Up to twenty children, ranging in age from two to five, can be served at the center, which the director hopes will provide the children with a stable environment, plus opportunities for educational and physical development.

Marian Wright Edelman, who heads the Children's Defense Fund, noted at the Kidspace dedication ceremony that for homeless families, especially families headed by homeless women, "child care spells work and self-sufficiency." Edelman pointed out that parents who struggle to complete job training and get jobs, must find a great deal of comfort knowing "that their children are safe and well cared for at Kidspace." [6]

7

Intergenerational Care

It has been called the first of its kind in the nation. It is the Intergenerational Day Care Center, a facility serving preschoolers and elderly people who are dependent. Located on the fourth floor of the Stride Rite Corporation headquarters in Cambridge, Massachusetts, the center includes separate sections for children and adults and a common meeting room where youngsters and old folks can get together for such events as a birthday party, reading activities, board games, and just socializing. Although the well-known children's shoe company has operated a child-care center since 1970, it opened its pioneer intergenerational facility in February 1990 and has been garnering tributes and widespread publicity ever since.

What is so special about the Intergenerational Day Care Center? It provides services that an increasing number of workers need—care not only for children but also for elderly family members who have disabilities or are too frail to stay home alone all day.

Why the Need for Elder Care?

Businesses across the country are finding that they must address the changing needs of families and the issue of elder care. Why? Primarily

81

because the number of eighteen-year-old workers in the nation is dropping, and many people in their thirties and older are entering the labor force. Older workers are likely to be responsible for the care of elderly patients, as well as for their children. As a result, workers may have to take time off work to care for both young and old dependent family members.

Because women are the primary caregivers, elder care is expected to be a major feminist issue of the 1990s, noted a report from the Older Women's League, a national organization that studies and works on behalf of older women's issues. The league found that about 89 percent of American women over age eighteen will provide care for children or parents or both. Over 30 percent will care for children and parents at the same time.

"On average, women today spend seventeen years of their lives caring for children and eighteen years assisting aged parents. For the first time ever, American couples have more parents than children. [The average intact nuclear family with two parents includes only one or two children.] The result will be a significant decline in the number of family caregivers at the same time the need increases dramatically," the report stated.

Statistics show how fast the number of elderly are increasing. About one out of eight Americans is over age sixty-five, and by the year 2000 around 35 million will be in that age group. Those over age seventy-five topped 10 million in the early 1980s and will increase to 17.2 million by the turn of the century. The fastest growing group in the United States are the elderly over eighty-five, expected to total about 5 million by 2000. A study prepared for a U.S. Senate Committee on Aging shows that about one-fourth of those over age sixty-five and half of the population over eighty-five need some kind of help, whether in dressing or other personal tasks, doing household chores, managing money, paying bills, or getting to the grocery store.

A variety of programs supported with tax funds or private donations help many elderly people live independently in their own homes. For example, volunteers in communities across the United

States operate Meals-on-Wheels programs, taking hot meals to seniors who may have problems buying or preparing their own food. Religious and social service groups often organize volunteers to make telephone calls to older people who are unable to leave their homes or to visit and do errands for shut-ins. Many communities provide low-cost or free transportation services for elderly citizens. Support groups and senior centers also provide for many of the social needs of the elderly.

Yet if older people become ill or disabled and need care or supervision during the day, how do they manage? Most do not want to live in nursing homes or with their adult children. In fact, the Senate committee study found that only 5 percent of the elderly population that are frail, chronically ill, or disabled live in nursing homes while another 5 percent live with their adult children or other family members. The rest live in their own homes and are cared for by family members or volunteer and/or paid caregivers.

In recent years, an increasing number of adult day-care centers have been offering care for the frail or disabled elderly. Such day care, in turn, helps family members who are the primary caregivers but need a brief respite from the responsibilities of providing constant care. An estimated 2,000 adult day-care centers are operating across the United States, and that number is increasing. In fact, one entrepreneur on the East Coast, Maurice Thompson, Jr., is in the process of developing a chain of Adult Day Clubs of America—a term Thompson feels is more dignified and presents the image of the elderly being treated as adults not children. The corporation that operates Kinder-Care also began a chain of ElderCare centers, opening twelve facilities in Texas in the summer of 1990.

Some adult day-care centers are geared toward social activities and may be located in churches or temples or facilities that are part of social service agencies. Usually those who go to social centers have only minor medical problems and can take part in crafts, discussions, and exercise programs. Adults with severe health problems such as crippling arthritis or Alzheimer's disease may be cared for at centers connected with hospitals or nursing homes, where registered nurses and other medical personnel can tend to clients' needs. But those who need care usually stay only during the day or, if the center has flexible hours, during the time period when their adult children or other family members are on the job.

Adult Care—Another Employee Benefit?

Since few adults are home to care for aging parents or other relatives, the need for elder care is becoming acute, experts say. In a 1989 survey, the American Association of Retired Persons (AARP) and the Travelers Foundation found that out of the seven million Americans who care for dependent parents, 12 percent have had to quit their jobs, and 14 percent worked part time so that they would be able to provide care for elderly family members.

According to an economist at Rutgers University, companies may have to provide employee benefits that help with care of elderly family members along with care of children. By offering elder-care benefits, companies will be able to obtain and keep a stable work force during the labor shortages expected during the 1990s.

Some companies already help employees set up support groups and bring in counselors and other professionals to discuss problems of dealing with older family members who are dependent. Other firms offer the Dependent Care Assistance Program, the federal program that allows companies to set aside funds that can be used tax-free for care of employees' children or dependent adults. Some companies will pay a portion of the cost of adult care. Family leave programs and flextime, the company benefits that aid in child care, also help families caring for frail or disabled elderly.

"The most common way that companies help employees to care for elderly relatives is through information and referral services," according to *Industry Week*. Usually such a service is modeled after child care R & Rs. In 1988, IBM started Elder Care Referral Services (ECRS), which includes 175 organizations nationwide that provide elder-care consultation and referrals. ECRS was developed by

Work/Family Elder Directions, a Boston, Massachusetts, firm, for IBM's 270,000 employees and retirees, but the service is available to other companies as well. Companies pay the costs of ECRS, but employees, retirees, or elderly relatives pay for the services of caregivers.[1]

Referral services often help employees whose elderly parents live far away. At a large international company like IBM, an employee working in a corporate facility in California, for example, can call a network of caseworkers. An employee can get advice about aid for a parent who lives across the country on the East Coast. A caseworker can provide such services as transporting a dependent parent to the doctor, helping a disabled adult adapt his or her home to a wheelchair, or even helping find a nursing home if needed.

Combining Care for Kids and Elders

Stride Rite's intergenerational care center located at a workplace is unique in the business world, and the on-site center may be a model for many major companies in the future. However, programs combining care for kids and elders are not new. They have been operating at various sites—urban, suburban, and rural—throughout the nation in such settings as nursing homes, housing complexes for the elderly, and adult day-care centers.

For example, in Junction City, Kansas, a child-care program called Wee Care is located at the Valley View Professional Care Center. The child-care center was designed to provide for children of employees working at the nursing home. But it now serves families in the community as well. Most parents choose the center because of its connection with the nursing home. Many of the children do not have grandparents close by, but the nursing home offers children social contact with the elderly.[2]

Not all nursing home residents enjoy being around children, but in many cases being with children energizes elders, and kids have an opportunity to be with grandparent-type people. At many nursing homes across the United States, intergenerational activities are part of the regular routine. Directors of such programs often point out that day care at a nursing home location helps children see that old age is part of life. Youngsters who may be afraid of people with disabilities soon learn to see older folks as people first.

The Oak and Acorn Day Care Center in Minneapolis, Minnesota, is part of a facility that offers only infant care in a nursery wing and serves only women residents at the nursing home. Many of the residents are volunteer "grandmas" who come to the nursery to hold, coo-and-cuddle the children while rocking them, to help feed and play "pat-a-cake" with those in high chairs, to play rolling games with large rubber beach balls, or to take the children outdoors in strollers. Staff at the day-care center sometimes take one-year-olds in a wagon, built with protective sides, on a trip through the halls of the nursing home, visiting residents in wheelchairs.

Another nursing home site near Phillipsburg, New Jersey, is the location for an after-school program serving children in grades one through three. The director of the after-school program works with the activities director of the nursing home to plan and carry out activities that the youngsters and oldsters can enjoy together. Some examples: they take part in gardening projects, an intergenerational choir, and a weekly bingo game.

Day-care centers connected with retirement complexes, adult-care facilities, or senior centers may offer child care for a full range of children, from babies to latchkey kids. Programs are designed to bring children and the elderly together for a variety of activities. For example, preschool children may join seniors to take part in religious celebrations or craft activities or to prepare and eat lunch together. They may get together to play board games or to hear stories. Seniors may help school-age children with homework, or children may share projects they have completed in classrooms.

The Foundation for Long Term Care, which conducts research and educational programs designed to improve the quality of life for the frail elderly, conducted a study of fifty-one preschool child-care programs located in long-term care facilities. In a report titled *Child*

In recent years, intergenerational centers have brought together young and old. Children in day-care programs often visit the elderly in nursing homes.

Care in Long Term Care Settings, the foundation noted that most of the shared activities in intergenerational programs were not devised as "busy work" or just to give kids and old folks something to do. Instead, they are designed to help the children develop motor and cognitive skills and to help the elderly maintain their abilities. For example, in Des Plaines, Illinois, at Parkside Human Services, a combined child and adult day-care center, the coordinator for intergenerational activities brought together older folks and youngsters for a guessing game. The coordinator distributed foam cups covered with aluminum foil that had been punctured, asking each person to figure out what was in her or his cup. As the report explained:

> Elders sniffed and shook the cups, the children sniffed and shook, they discussed and guessed. The answers turned out to be strawberries, bananas, and apples. Cutting boards and plastic knives were distributed. Under close staff supervision, the fruits were cut up for a fruit salad snack. Children and elders enjoyed their snack together before the children returned to their area.

> This activity, involving sensory, analytical and fine motor skills . . . clearly stimulates and maintains the skills of the elderly, develops the skills of the children and is fun for all.[3]

Older People as Caregivers

Many older people, particularly those who live independently in senior residential centers or in public housing projects, take part in preschool programs and child-care programs for school-age children. Seniors usually serve as aides, either as volunteers or as paid workers. Although some older people do not relate well to children, most seniors have experiences to share and a way of looking at life that children might not learn about otherwise since many young people do not live close to their grandparents or other older extended-family members. Seniors also can offer children support and nurturing, which is sometimes in short supply because of changing family patterns.

In Milwaukee, Wisconsin, a community action agency sponsors a program called Juniors and Elders Together (JET) and has set up three after-school programs in inner city schools. Older folks go through a six-week training program and receive minimum wages to assist in various activities. Seniors may help preschoolers develop social skills and self-control, which in turn help the youngsters when they enroll in kindergarten or first grade. The senior aides also work with school-age children—tutoring or perhaps helping to supervise field trips or art projects or musical programs.

Bringing the generations together is one of the basic reasons for a child-care program on the campus of Northeastern Illinois University in Chicago. Two faculty members in the Education Department at the university, Barbara Lowenthal and Rosemary Egan, initiated the program in 1988, believing it would help the children prepare for elementary school and reduce the isolation of many older citizens. More than twenty seniors, whom the children call "grandpa" and "grandma," come to the center to read to the children, play games with them, and just plain have fun with the fifty youngsters enrolled.

In a survey of parents, senior citizens, and staff involved in the program, Lowenthal and Egan found that children improved their self-esteem and were more involved in story-reading activities. Seniors also gained, indicating that they enjoyed the children "very, very, very much," as one woman put it. Another pointed out that she felt "extremely welcome" and that a lot of love is expressed at the center. Most seniors said they were able to forget about aches and pains when taking part in activities with the children.[4]

Similar reactions come from intergenerational programs set up in other parts of the nation. In New Jersey, the state's Division on Aging supports several after-school programs for latchkey children, using volunteer senior citizens as aides. Seniors say that such programs "make me feel needed" or "not so lonely."

One New Jersey program is located in a community room of a public housing project in Plainfield. Another is in a rural area called

Egg Harbor Township and serves between sixty and eighty children whose parents work outside the home. According to a report in *Aging*, a journal published by the U.S. Department of Health and Human Services, the children:

> . . . are bused after classes to the Davenport School where the program is held. Senior aides also have the option of riding the school bus. With full use of several classrooms, the library, gym and other school facilities, the program offers arts and crafts, cooking projects, bowling and field trips.

Supervisors of the program say that the children "adore the older adults as they would their own grandparents." And one sixth grader said that he had made a lot of friends while in the program and that being there after school was "a lot better than going home and having nothing to do, or just watching TV." [5]

Craft projects are often part of after-school programs for elementary school students. In Plainfield, New Jersey, a program set up through state funding brings together young and old as seniors help youngsters with a variety of activities.

8

The Bottom Line—Is Day Care Really Good for Kids?

Countless working parents have described the benefits of having quality care available for their children or other dependent family members. One mother who had used the services of a baby-sitter decided that a day-care center was much more beneficial for her three-year-old daughter because "she needed friends to play with and she's learned a lot."

Mark Woodmore takes his five-year-old to a day-care facility connected with the St. Joseph Medical Center in South Bend, Indiana. Mark works at the hospital, and the day-care facility is across the street. His remarks are typical of parents who are enthusiastic about day care, particularly on-the-job day care:

> I feel the hospital really has gone a long way to develop a quality day-care center. The teachers help make my daughter blossom. She's a bright little girl, and day-care programs "tease" her brain—I mean she's being stimulated to learn. She's learned to count to fifty, she knows the alphabet, and she's learned to

cooperate—how to be among her peers and get along with them. She's found out she can't get her own way all the time.

One example to show how she's learned—I was rushing to get ready to go to work one morning and she was getting dressed—which she has learned to do by herself, by the way—but we were running behind, so I told her to "come on, hurry up, we've got to go." She started to sing a song she'd learned at day care, "Patience is a virtue." She taught Daddy something that day!

Another thing—my daughter really likes day care—all she wants to do is go back. When I was on vacation for a week, she was upset. She was happy when I told her I had to go back to work—her comment was, "Yea! I get to go to school." [1]

Yet some parents and child development experts are highly critical of day care, particularly for infants. Some believe that infants (up to the age of one year) placed in day care become insecure and can develop psychological problems later in life, becoming anxious and aggressive. The children may have difficulty relating to their peers and adults as they get older.

Surveys of more than 1,400 pediatricians—one conducted by the Thomas Jefferson University School of Medicine and another by the American Academy of Pediatrics—found that a majority of those polled believed child care by someone other than an infant's mother could be detrimental for babies. Many believe mothers should care for their babies at home until the children are at least six months of age.

However, pediatricians nationwide point out that there are only a few long-term studies upon which to base their views. There are also many factors to consider—such as family values, approaches to parenting, and the financial question of whether a mother can afford to stay home. As Dr. Antoinette Eaton, vice president of the American Academy of Pediatrics, explained to a reporter: "There is no question in my mind that the economic benefits of a mother's working are going to help a child who might otherwise be raised in poverty." [2]

Mark Woodmore has nothing but praise for the day-care center that his daughter, Cherrelle, attends. Here he prepares to leave Cherrelle at the gate of the center which is operated by the hospital where Mark works.

✳ Experts Debate Effects of Day Care

During the 1950s and 1960s, child-care professionals were warning parents that children separated from their parents for long periods of time (as in full-time day care) would suffer emotional problems later in life. Such a blanket prediction for all day-care enrollees has proven false. But over the past decade, experts in child development have been arguing over the effects of day care on parent-child bonding, a term specialists use to describe the attachment or close relationship that develops between an infant and parent (usually the mother). According to the bonding theory, if the infant-mother bond is secure, the child will be able to develop as a confident, trusting individual. On the other hand, when bonding does not take place or is broken, the child could have adjustment problems later on.

One of the methods used to determine whether parent-infant bonding is secure is the "Strange Situation" test. During the testing, observers watch infants through a one-way glass or the children are videotaped. Babies are left alone or with a stranger for a set period of time, and when the mother returns, observers record how the infant responds. Simply put, if a baby reacts joyfully when reunited with her or his Mom, the observer labels the child "secure." If the child ignores Mom, observers judge the baby "anxious-avoidant," or one likely to be insecure.

Jay Belsky, of Pennsylvania State University, long has been researching infants in day care and is considered one of the nation's top authorities on the subject. During his studies in the 1970s, Belsky concluded that day care had no adverse effects on children, but in later research and analyses of other studies he reversed his opinion. According to his writings and testimony before congressional committees looking into family issues, Belsky now concludes that infants who spend more than twenty hours per week in a day-care center, in a family day-care home, or in the home being cared for by a nanny, housekeeper, or baby-sitter are at risk. The infants may become hyperactive or develop emotional problems.[3]

In a recent essay, Belsky notes that repeated studies have shown:

> . . . that children who experienced full-time nonparental care in the first year of life are more likely to appear, at the end of their first year, insecure in their attachment to their parents and, between the third and tenth years of life, more disobedient and aggressive than children whose day care was initiated after their first year.[4]

Belsky makes it clear that not every child who grows up in a family relying on nonparental care for more than twenty hours per week is doomed to behavior problems, and "it is totally inappropriate to conclude that only mothers can care for their infants or that day care is bad for babies." But he notes that the findings regarding nonparental care for infants give him "serious cause for concern." Since an increasing number of infants are cared for by someone other than parents, Belsky urges increased parental leaves from jobs to care for newborns and a national effort to develop affordable, quality child-care facilities.[5]

T. Berry Brazelton, a nationally known psychiatrist and pediatrician and author of best-selling books on child care, generally supports the theory that the period after birth is a crucial time for establishing the mother-infant bond. But he also emphasizes that the ideal of mothers staying at home to care for children is not working for 70 to 80 percent of the families in the United States, and parents who work outside the home and have to leave their children with substitute caregivers feel guilt and grief. To deal with their reactions, parents may become detached, not because they "don't care, but because it hurts so much to care." Brazelton believes parents should not blame themselves for feeling anxious and guilty but receive support in finding the best possible care for their children.[6]

Few argue about the need for consistent, high-quality care for children. But some specialists believe that secure parent-child bonding depends on many variables, not primarily on whether a mother stays home to care for her child. According to some theories, the attachment between parent and child may be affected by such factors as the mother's self-esteem (or lack of it), the way the mother was treated as a child and how that has affected her personality, the marital relationship (whether it affects the mother in positive or negative ways), and so on. Sandra Scarr, of the University of Virginia and author of *Mother Care—Other Care*, contends that even if infants who have been in nonparental care exhibit emotional problems, they are minor difficulties and usually can be rectified in a short time.

Another criticism of the infant-bonding theory is that few studies have concentrated on infant-father attachments and what impact that kind of bonding has on a child's development. Most research begins with the accepted theory that a baby's relationship with its mother determines how the child will develop emotionally and relate to others later in life.

One long-term study by researcher Carollee Howes at the University of California at Los Angeles looked at how eighty children, who had been enrolled in day care as infants, adjusted to kindergarten. Published in 1990, the study found behavior patterns similar to those described by Belsky. "Children who entered low-quality child care as infants had the most difficulty with peers as preschoolers . . . " Howes wrote. She pointed out that teachers said the children were easily distracted, less task-oriented, and more hostile. However, Howes concluded: "Only those children enrolled as infants in low-quality, as opposed to high-quality, child-care centers, appeared maladjusted." Howes added that "children who entered high-quality child care as infants did not appear different from the children who entered high-quality care as older children." [7]

Child development experts generally agree that substitute care for older children is seldom harmful *if* quality care is available. In a "Letters to the Editor" column of the *Washington Post*, Marjorie Barnett, a pediatrician practicing in Washington, D.C., explained that 75 percent of the children she sees have working mothers and many of the children attend day care. Dr. Barnett pointed out:

> The vast majority of the children I see who go to centers are taken care of with warmth and affection in hygienic surroundings. This is partly because their parents are able to afford the cost of better day care centers and partly because of the level of sophistication in the Washington area concerning care of children.
>
> . . . In my practice, where we see thousands of children a year, most children profit from their day care experience as a result of having involved, caring parents who are fortunate to be able to discriminate among some fairly high-quality providers. I worry more about the many children who are not as fortunate and must go to centers where standards are minimal and which require a higher degree of health and safety regulation.[8]

As the varied opinions of experts show, child-care issues are complex, and many questions about the effects of nonparental care have yet to be answered. In an attempt to reach more definite conclusions about how day care affects children and families, the National Institute of Child Health and Development launched a five-year study, beginning in 1990. Called the National Study of Young Children's Lives, it is being conducted by ten research facilities in various parts of the nation. Researchers are following the development of at least 1,200 children, beginning at the age of one month to three years old, who are in varied types of day care. The youngsters come from diverse economic and social backgrounds and family structures.

What do the researchers hope to learn? A primary goal is to find evidence upon which to draw conclusions about how infants are affected by care outside the home. Researchers also want to know what effect day care has on children's social, emotional, and mental development. They expect to learn whether day care helps youngsters become more or less independent and the impact of day care on family relationships.

Health Hazards at Day-Care Centers?

Along with investigating psychological problems that might occur with children in full-time day care, some research has been conducted on various health problems associated with child-care centers. Outbreaks of colds, flu, and digestive tract illnesses such as diarrhea are more common among children in day care than those who stay at home. Chicken pox also spreads quickly among children in day-care facilities.

Why are children in day-care centers targets for such diseases? The primary reason is the number of children in close quarters and the fact that staff may not follow strict procedures for control of infections. According to specialists in pediatric diseases, staff always need to wash their hands after diapering babies, after changing clothing that has been soiled by sick children, after wiping noses, and certainly before any food preparation. Health experts say that infection-control measures also should include daily use of a chlorine bleach solution to disinfect such surfaces as diaper-changing areas, tables and chairs, and bathroom fixtures. Plastic toys need daily baths as well. And when children become sick at a day-care facility, they should be isolated from others until they can go home.

Another health problem that has become common in day-care facilities is head lice. Lice used to be a problem associated only with the poor and dirty. But with so many children together, lice can quickly spread if precautions are not taken. To prevent infestations, day-care centers (and some state laws) usually require that each baby have its own crib and each child have her or his own mat or cot for resting. Regulations prohibit sharing combs, brushes, pillows, and similar personal items. Coat hooks are twelve to eighteen inches apart to prevent lice from spreading.

If a day-care teacher or aide discovers a child with lice, every child needs to be examined, and parents should be notified. Most centers do not allow infested children to return to a day-care facility until they are free of the pests. When caught early, head lice can be treated easily with medications found on drugstore shelves or with prescriptions from doctors. Bed linens need to be washed and furniture, car seats, and stuffed animals vacuumed thoroughly. The Centers for Disease Control, a federal agency, advises against pesticide sprays that may be toxic to children.

Day-care centers must also guard against injuries to young children, although the rate of injury in licensed day-care facilities is lower than in children's own homes. A study conducted in Atlanta, Georgia, looked at seventy-one facilities—day-care centers, preschools, and learning centers—serving 5,300 children in the Greater Atlanta area.

Researchers found that facilities reported 143 injuries, which included cuts, fractures, and human bites, severe enough for the child to require medical or dental care. Two-year-olds had the highest injury rate. Nearly half of the injuries, as might be expected, occurred on the playground, and most were the result of falls. The researchers suggested that safety improvements at day-care centers "should focus on the playground" with the use of "impact-absorbing surfaces" that could help reduce injuries.

What Parents Say

While health and child development specialists study how children are affected by nonparental care, parents have their own ideas on the subject. A number of nationally distributed magazines and major newspapers have conducted surveys of readers, asking for opinions on child care. Although responses come primarily from mothers, fathers also expressed their views.

Overall, parents say that given the best of all possible situations, both mother and father should share in child care to provide optimal nurturing and to encourage children's development. But no family functions perfectly or exists in a perfect world. Differences of opinion arise when parents tell how they feel families should handle child care under less-than-ideal conditions.

Parents who are generally opposed to substitute care of children (outside the home or in the home) say that families should cut back on their wants so that both parents do not have to work. That may mean sacrifices, but it is worth giving up things to see that children develop and grow in a healthy manner, some parents say. A father who decided to be the prime parent during his child's first year, put it this way: "I loved being with my daughter and taking an active part in her daily life. I was able to experience the joy of my own child—meeting her needs became my needs." [9]

Mothers who agree with this view usually report—with some satisfaction and pride—that they have given up jobs in order to have more time with their young children. Those who work part time say that their lives are more balanced because they are able to be home when their children need them. To many mothers, rearing children is an important career that can be highly creative and rewarding.

Comments printed in a variety of publications make it clear that some at-home mothers believe that working mothers are selfish and only pursuing careers to buy more and more consumer goods. They sometimes express resentment that working mothers do not take their share of responsibility for such functions as school programs, children's sports activities, and volunteer work for religious and civic organizations.

But mothers who choose to stay home are not always satisfied with their roles. Some complain about the lack of stimulation and worry about what they will do when their children are grown and gone. [10]

On the other side of the fence, many working mothers say they resent being forced to choose between a career and staying home. Many find it painful to leave their young children. They are frequently frustrated when a day-care provider is the one who experiences, for example, their baby's first smile or recognizable word or their toddler's first step.

Those who have earned degrees and work in professions from advertising to nursing to law say they love their families and love their work too. "Why," asked a nurse, "can't I provide a needed service and also have good care for my children who understand why I do what I do?" [11]

Working mothers sometimes bristle when their jobs outside the home are equated with self-interest. In two-wage-earner families, mothers say they need the income that both parents earn in order to pay for basic needs. Single mothers in particular feel that critics are unfair when they imply that mothers working outside the home are not being "good" parents. Most have no other alternative except welfare. As one single mother said: "You're damned if you work and damned if you don't work. I do the best I can, and I'm with my children several hours every day after work and always on the weekend. I think we're doing okay."

9

Finding Quality Child Care

> We're moving this summer, and I must take my daughter out of
> her day-care center and find another one. I know this is necessary,
> but I constantly worry whether the new center will be as good as
> her present one . . .[1]

The parent writing about this problem wanted to know what she could do to relieve her anxiety, posing her question for a newspaper advice column called "Working Parents." Because there are no national standards for child-care facilities or providers, parents across the United States are looking for information on how to find quality child care. As a result, tips on child care appear not only in newspaper columns but also in magazines ranging from *American Baby* to *Boston Magazine* to *Changing Times*.

Books also cover the subject. Danalee Buhler's *The Very Best Child Care and How to Find It* is one resource. (See **Further Reading** for others.) State day-care licensing agencies, child welfare departments, social service agencies, and child-care resource and referral services can help. Teachers and administrators may have suggestions about programs for after-school care.

Those who provide information on child care may be able to help identify the kind of child care parents need, want, and can afford—one of the first steps toward problem-solving. Parents may have to decide whether to use the services of a baby-sitter, live-in nanny or housekeeper, a family day-care provider in the neighborhood, a day-care center, nursery, preschool, learning center, or school-based program. Of course a choice would depend on what services are actually available in a community.

Finding Care for an Infant

As all the medical and child-care experts will emphasize, babies need a lot of individual attention and consistent care. Most parents usually prefer to have one person on a regular basis provide care for their infants. Perhaps that means taking a child to a baby-sitter or having a sitter, professional nanny, or au pair come to the home. Professional agencies such as Nannies Network and AuPairCare screen people who serve as nannies or au pairs, and parents can interview any prospective caregiver before making a decision about hiring. But when it comes to hiring a nonprofessional baby-sitter, parents usually have to make the judgments—find a person they can trust to care for their child.

Some gruesome stories have emerged regarding unqualified sitters, some of whom neglect or abuse children. But, as with child-care providers in centers, it is rare that baby-sitters harm children in their care. Nevertheless, unless the sitter has been recommended by relatives, friends, or neighbors, parents should find out about a sitter's experience, ask for references, and talk to people who have hired the sitter on a regular basis.

When a sitter has been hired, parents need to spend some time with the sitter and child to note care-giving techniques. Parents also should explain what is expected of a sitter—make clear what the hours and duties are. For some sitters, it may be necessary to set limits on the use of the telephone, smoking, having friends visit, and even on TV watching if it interferes with safe child care. It is important, as well, that a sitter know how to cope with medical and other emergencies.

Family day care or a day-care center may be the choice for parents of infants, particularly if babies receive individual attention. What should parents look for in such facilities?

The ratio of adults to children is one important aspect. In family day care, the provider should have no more than five or six children, including her own, and only two infants among them. In a day-care center, one adult caregiver should be available for every three or four babies, and each baby should have a primary person caring for her or him.

The baby should be with the same caregiver for the first year since turnover is one of the greatest threats to the quality of infant care, experts say. Some studies—one in the Boston area in particular—show that nonprofit day-care centers are less likely to have turnover than for-profit centers. Caregivers should interact with the babies, holding them while they are bottle-fed, talking to them during diaper and clothing changes, and rocking or holding them when they need comforting.

Pediatricians and child development specialists urge parents to ask leading questions when looking at facilities for infant or older child care. Some examples:

—How much are teachers and aides paid? (Their salaries may determine whether or not the day-care facility has a high turnover rate.)

—How long have employees worked with children. Have they received any training in early childhood development?

—Will the caregiver share information about infants with their parents? (Parents need to know how their children are doing without having to press for information or feel intimidated by staff.)

—Can parents visit or call whenever they feel the need to check on their children?

—Who inspects the facility and how often?

Checking Out Day Care for Preschoolers

Some of the same questions apply to facilities providing care for preschoolers. Almost every advice article or how-to book on finding child care includes a list of questions or a checklist to guide the search. Usually there are a number of different categories to evaluate.

One aspect to investigate is sanitation and cleanliness. Diaper-changing areas should be located well away from the food preparation area, for example. Of course, the staff should wash their hands after changing diapers or helping older children use the toilet. Children also should be encouraged to wash their hands regularly. As described in the previous chapter, surface areas should be cleaned and disinfected frequently to prevent the spread of infections.

Safety measures are important. Parents can check the facility to see whether dangerous tools, poisonous cleaning products, and other hazardous materials are out of the children's reach. Are there smoke detectors and fire extinguishers, and what about an exit plan in case of fire or other emergency precautions? A list of emergency phone numbers should be posted near the phone. Does the facility keep medical records for each child? Do staff members know first aid? Can at least one person administer cardiopulmonary resuscitation (CPR) and the Heimlich maneuver?

Parents frequently express concern about child abuse. Even though statistics clearly show that abuse is more common in a child's home or the home of a relative or friend than in a day-care facility, parents should find out whether they can drop in unannounced at any time to see how a facility is operating. If parents are unable to visit, they should be able to send friends or relatives. For security, day-care providers should have a method for screening strangers. Do they have to sign in? No stranger should be allowed to roam the premises. Does the provider check out the person who picks up a child at the end of the day?

Some signs to alert parents to possible abuse are described in Danalee Buhler's book. She cautions that the media coverage of

106

notorious abuse cases has misled some parents, who may misinterpret hugs and kisses. As Buhler put it: "Infants and toddlers need lots of hugs and kisses as part of the nurturing process, especially when forming new attachments and dealing with the stress of separation from parents."

Buhler, who operated a day-care center, also advises parents to find out what caregivers consider appropriate methods of discipline. As she explained:

> Many caregivers of infants and toddlers believe in slapping the back of a child's hand, swatting a diapered bottom, or spanking as appropriate discipline. I believe, like many child care professionals, that hitting a child only reinforces his/her belief that you consider hitting an appropriate way of dealing with a situation . . . When you discipline children, you are teaching them how to respond to a certain situation. Punishment is the intentional infliction of pain, whether emotional or physical.[2]

Instead of corporal punishment, child development experts suggest the use of "time-outs," or having children sit quietly until they can calm down and behave appropriately with others.

Parents can ask many questions about activities, routines, and schedules, such as what kinds of meals and snacks are served and when; do the children go on field trips and, if so, what kind of safety measures are taken; are there structured learning activities as well as free playtime?

One of the most important aspects for parents to observe is how caregivers interact with children. Child-care specialists suggest that parents note whether providers listen to children and give youngsters attention and comfort when needed. How do caregivers handle children who fight? How much time does the provider spend directly with the children? Parents also should heed their own instincts. If parents are uncomfortable with a day-care provider or if children consistently show they are unhappy with caregivers, it is probably best to find another day-care home or center.

Nutritious snacks are an important part of the day-care routine.

Will Quality Child Care Be Available in the Future?

Early in 1990 the National Academy of Sciences (NAS) issued a report on child care, which had been developed over a two-year period for the U.S. Department of Health and Human Services. Titled "Who Cares for America's Children?," the report emphasized the need for standards for child-care providers and pointed out that quality child care can provide a significant boost to poor children. John L. Palmer, chairman of the NAS panel, explained:

> We found substantial scientific evidence of a strong tie between the quality of care a child receives early in life and healthy development of that child's cognitive skills and social relationships . . . out-of-home child care can offset to some extent the detrimental effects on development of a stressful impoverished home environment. The bottom line of this research is that quality matters in child care.[3]

But with no national standards for child care and a patchwork system of child-care providers, no one can make predictions about the quality of child-care facilities in the years ahead. Generally, specialists in the field are calling for more activism on the part of parents and more widespread education about the need for quality child care, which can benefit the public good just as investment in a public school system helps educate a majority of citizens not just an elite few. The experts believe that more pressure will be applied on employers to provide child-and elder-care benefits and that schools systems and local governments will become more involved in child-care programs.

Quality child care also will depend on whether trained caregivers receive adequate pay for their work. Rarely does a person want to obtain higher education and accept a job making less than he or she can make at a car wash or fast-food restaurant.

Finally, the United States must decide as a nation whether child care will have a high priority. As one member of the U.S. Congress pointed out, in many cases it appears that more attention is given to farm animals than to children. The federal standards set for the feeding and care of pigs, cattle, dairy, cows, and poultry far outnumber those set for child care. If Americans truly believe that children are the nation's "most precious resources," then a well-planned and clear national policy for child care seems long overdue.

Notes by Chapter

Chapter 1

1. As projected by Sandra L. Hofferth, "What Is the Demand for and Supply of Child Care in the United States?" *Young Children* (July 1989), p. 29.

2. "Preventing U.S. Infant Deaths," *Population Today,* (April 1990), p. 9.

3. Sidebar statistics, *Newsweek*, special edition, (Winter/Spring 1990), p. 49.

4. Jonathan Kozol, "The New Untouchables," *Newsweek*, special edition, (Winter/Spring 1990), p. 52.

5. Sandra Evans, "No One to Watch Over Them," *Washington Post,* (October 21, 1990), p. A1.

Chapter 2

1. As quoted by Margaret O'Brien Steinfels, *Who's Minding the Children* (New York: Simon & Schuster, 1973), p. 36.

2. Alfred Kadushin, "Substitute Care: Foster Family Care," *Child Welfare Services* (New York: Macmillan, 1980), pp. 315–320.

3. Douglas R. Powell, "Day Care As a Family Support System," *America's Family Support Program* (New Haven, Conn. and London: Yale University Press, 1987), pp. 115–116.

4. Gerald F. Kreyche, "Day Care: The New Surrogacy," *USA Today,* Magazine, (September 1989), p. 93.

5. Alison Leigh Cowan, "Poll Finds Women's Gains Have Been Taking a Personal Toll," *The New York Times,* (August 21, 1989), p. A14.

6. Sandra L. Hofferth, "What Is the Demand for and Supply of Child Care in the United States?" *Young Children,* (July 1989), p. 33.

7. Sheila B. Kamerman, "Child Care, Women, Work, and the Family: An International Overview of Child Care Services and Related Policies," *Caring for Children: Challenge to America* (Hillsdale, N.J. and London: Lawrence Erlbaum Associates, 1989), p. 107.

8. Robin Knight, "A Euro-solution: Send Toddlers to School," *U.S. News & Work Report,* (August 22, 1988), pp. 33–34.

9. As quoted in *The Oregonian,* (December 31, 1989), p. A2.

10. Julie Rovner, "Congress Wraps Up Decision on Child-Care Legislation," *Congressional Quarterly,* (October 27, 1990), p. 3605.

Chapter 3

1. Sandra L. Hofferth, "What Is the Demand for and Supply of Child Care in the United States?" *Young Children,* (July 1989), p. 31.

2. As quoted by A. J. Dickerson (Associated Press), "So Many Yupppies, So Few Nannies," *San Francisco Chronicle,* (November 15, 1990), p. B6.

3. Robert J. Klein, "Finding Live-in Help for Your Child That Is Loving, Loyal and Also Legal," *Money,* (September 1989), p. 155.

4. Personal interview, (February 1990).

5. "States Inadequately Protect Children in Child Care," *CDF Reports,* (September 1990), p. 1.

6. Kathy Boccella, "The Battle Over Day-Care Homes," *Philadelphia Inquirer,* (November 23, 1989), p. H4.

7. Irene Nyborg-Andersen and Pamela Guthrie O'Brien, "The Child-Care Patchwork," *Ladies' Home Journal,* (November 1989), p. 200.

8. Telephone interview, May 1990.

9. As quoted by Sue Chastain, "A Century of Child Care," *Philadelphia Inquirer*, (October 29, 1989), p. I1.

10. News release, December 1989.

11. As quoted by Patrick T. Reardon, "Recognition Comes to Teacher Who's Devoted to Her Preschool," *Chicago Tribune*, (November 13, 1990), p. 5.

12. Personal Interview, April 1990.

Chapter 4

1. Telephone interview, February 1990.

2. Personal interview, February 1990.

3. Cindy Skrzycki, "Taking a First Step Toward Child Care," *Washington Post*, (October 30, 1990), p. D1.

4. Claudia H. Deutsch, "Getting Women Down to the Site," *The New York Times*, (March 11, 1990), Section 3, p. 25.

5. Patricia R. Collins, Paul Krause, and Sandra Machida, "Making Child Care an Employee Benefit," *Management Accounting*, (April 1990), p. 29.

6. Fran Sussner Rodgers and Charles Rodgers, "Business and the Facts of Family Life," *Harvard Business Review*, (November/December 1989), p. 126.

Chapter 5

1. Harold Howe, II, "Giving Equity a Chance in the Excellence Game" *The Great School Debate*, eds. Beatrice and Ronald Gross (New York: Simon & Schuster, 1985), p. 295.

2. Ronald Henkoff, "Now Everyone Loves Head Start," *Fortune*, Special Issue, (Spring 1990), p. 36.

3. "Preschool Programs: Lost Opportunity" (editorial), *Chicago Tribune*, (May 13, 1990), p. 2.

4. Connie Leslie and Karen Springen, "Schools That Never Close," *Newsweek*, (May 15, 1989), p. 60.

5. Edward B. Fiske, "Starting with a Center for Child Care, A School Welcomes Social Services for Families," *The New York Times*, (January 17, 1990), p. B8.

6. As quoted by Pamela McKuen, " 'Substitute Mom' Fills a Need," *Chicago Tribune*, (November 7, 1990), p. 64.

7. Joan G. Schine, "Adolescents Help Themselves by Helping Others," *Children Today*, (January/February 1989), p. 11.

8. Patricia Rowe, "Preventing Infant Mortality: An Investment in the Nation's Future," *Children Today*, (January/February 1989), pp. 16–17.

Chapter 6

1. Leah Y. Latimer, "For Parents of Disabled Children, Day-Care Problem Is Compounded," *Washington Post*, (November 28, 1989), p. E1.

2. Diego Ribadeneira, "Day Care Open to HIV Toddlers," *Boston Globe*, (June 21, 1989), p. 1.

3. Personal interview, (September 1989).

4. "Survivors of Abuse," *CAPS Newsletter*,(Fall 1988), entire issue.

5. Personal interview, January 1990.

6. As quoted by Jill Nelson, "Haven for Homeless Children Dedicated," *Washington Post*, (May 10, 1990), p. B1.

Chapter 7

1. Joani Nelson-Horchler, "Elder Care Comes of Age," *Industry Week*, (January 2, 1989), pp. 54–56.

2. Cheryl Tevis, "Old and Young Gain Mutual Benefits Under Same Roof," *Successful Farming*, (September 1989), p. 66.

3. Carol R. Hegeman, *Child Care in Long Term Care Settings* (Albany, N.Y.: Foundation for Long Term Care, 1985), p. 13.

4. Patrick T. Reardon, "Who's Watching the Kids?" *Chicago Tribune*, (April 29, 1990), p. 1.

5. "Brighter Afternoons for Latchkey Children," *Aging*, (Winter 1989), pp. 20–22.

Chapter 8

1. Personal interview, April 1990.

2. Shari Roan, "R_x Lacking in Day-Care Dilemma," *Los Angeles Times*, (May 22, 1990), p. E1.

3. Jay Belsky, "Infant-Parent Attachment and Day Care: In Defense of the Strange Situation", *Caring for Children: Challenge to America* (Hillsdale, N. J.: Lawrence Erlbaum Associates, 1989), pp. 23–47. Also see: Barbara F. Meltz, "Day Care for Infants: Look for a Loving Bond," *Boston Globe*, (December 15, 1989), Section 3, p. 101.

4. Jay Belsky, "Infant Day Care, Child Development, and Family Policy," *Society*, (August 1990), p. 11.

5. Ibid.

6. Speech by T. Berry Brazelton at the Century Center, South Bend, Indiana, February 26, 1990.

7. Carollee Howes, "Can the Age of Entry into Child Care and the Quality of Child Care Predict Adjustment in Kindergarten?" *Developmental Psychology*, (February 1990), p. 300.

8. Marjorie Barnett, "Care for Kids" (Letters to the Editor), *Washington Post,* (April 19, 1990), p. A26.

9. Personal interview, January 1988.

10. Paul Krantz, "Day Care: Are We Shortchanging Our Kids?" *Better Homes and Gardens,* (June 1989), pp. 20–22.

11. Personal interview, May 1990.

Chapter 9

1. Shelly Phillips, "Working Parents" (column), *Philadelphia Inquirer,* (April 29, 1990), p. J2.

2. Danalee Buhler, *The Very Best Child Care and How to Find It.* (Rocklin, Calif.: Prima Publishing, 1989), p. 126.

3. As quoted by Linda Kramer, "Teaching Congress the ABCs," *The Oregonian,* (April 8, 1990), p. B1.

Further Reading

Books

Buhler, Danalee. *The Very Best Child Care and How to Find It.* Rocklin, Calif.: Prima Publishing & Communications, 1989.

Gay, Kathlyn. *Changing Families: Meeting Today's Challenges.* Hillside, N.J.: Enslow Publishers, 1988.

Hegeman, Carol R. *Child Care in Long Term Care Settings.* Albany, N.Y.: Foundation for Long Term Care, Inc., 1985.

Hubbard, April, and Clementine Hayburn. *Day Care Parenting.* New York: First Bart Books, 1985.

Lande, Jeffrey S., Sandra Scarr, and Nina Guzenhauser, eds. *Caring for Children: Challenge to America.* Hillsdale, N.J., and London: Lawrence Erlbaum Associates, 1989.

National Research Council. *Who Cares for America's Children.* Washington, D.C.: National Academy Press, 1990.

Pittman, Karen. *Preventing Children Having Children.* Washington, D.C.: Children's Defense Fund, 1985.

Steinfels, Margaret O'Brien. *Who's Minding the Children?* New York: Simon & Schuster, 1973.

Zinsser, Caroline, and Betsy Andrews. *One Hundred Working Women: Balancing Employment and Child Care.* New York: Center for Public Advocacy Research, 1988.

Articles

Becker, Gary S. "Sure, Spend More on Child Care. But Spend Wisely." *Business Week*, May 8, 1989, p. 24.

Bellm, Dan. "The McChild-Care Empire." *Mother Jones*, April 1987, pp. 32–38.

Belsky, Jay. "Infant Day Care, Child Development, and Family Policy." *Society*, July/August 1990, pp. 10–12.

Berger, Joseph. "New York Plans Workplace Schools." *The New York Times*, March 7, 1990, p. B6.

Bloom, David E., and Todd Steen. "Why Childcare Is Good for Business." *American Demographics*, August 1988 (reprint, no page numbers).

Brazelton, T. Berry. "First Steps: Working Through the Lives of Children." *The World*, March/April 1989, pp. 10–11.

———. "Nurturing the Nurturers." *World Monitor*, March 1989, pp. 14–17.

———. "Working Parents." *Newsweek*, February 13, 1989, pp. 66–72.

Brophy, Beth. "Corporate Nannies for a New Decade." *U.S. News & World Report*, December 25, 1989 / January 1, 1990, pp. 70–72.

Caldwell, Bettye. "Day Care Family Style." *American Baby*, August 1989, pp. 60, 71–72.

Carlson, Allan. "Family Questions." *Society*, July/August 1990, pp. 4–6.

Children's Defense Fund. "States Inadequately Protect Children in Child Care." *CDF Reports*, September 1990, pp. 1–2.

Clark, Marc, Lisa Van Dusen, and Deborra Schug. "The New Day Care Policy," *Macleans*, December 14, 1987, pp. 14–16.

Cohen, Deborah L. "In Unusual Business Deal, St. Paul Opens Kindergarten, Day-Care Center at Bank." *Education Week,* September 6, 1989, p. 7.

———. "Postponement of Child-Care Bill Spurs Fears About Its Prospects." *Education Week,* November 22, 1989, p. 1.

Cohn, Bob. "A Glimpse of the 'Flex' Future." *Newsweek,* August 1, 1988, pp. 38–39.

———. "How to Help the Working Poor." *Newsweek,* August 7, 1989, p. 26.

Collins, Patricia R., Paul Krause, and Sandra Machida. "Making Child Care an Employee Benefit." *Management Accounting,* April 1990, pp. 26–29.

Cotton, Sandra, John K. Antill, and John D. Cunningham. "The Work Motivations of Mothers With Preschool Children." *Journal of Family Issues,* June 1989, pp. 189–209.

Cowan, Alison Leigh. "Women's Gains on the Job: Not Without a Heavy Toll." *The New York Times,* August 21, 1989, pp. A1, A4.

Darnton, Nina. "Mommy Vs. Mommy." *Newsweek,* June 4, 1990, pp. 64–67.

"Day Care for the Elderly." *U.S. News & World Report,* September 12, 1988, p. 73.

"Department of Labor Report." *Congressional Digest,* February 1990, pp. 34–35.

Deutsch, Claudia H. "Getting Women Down to the Site." *The New York Times,* March 11, 1990, p. F25.

Dowling, Claudia Glenn. "Old Hands: Who's Minding the Kids? Who's Helping the Old Folks?" *Life,* December 1989, pp. 102–103.

Dreyfous, Leslie. "Duties Heaped on Moms Who Return to Jobs." Associated Press feature, November 11, 1990.

Ehrenreich, Barbara, and Deirdre English. "Blowing the Whistle on the 'Mommy Track.' " *Ms.* July/August 1989, pp. 56–58.

Evans, Sandra. "Study Urges Higher Pay for Day-Care Workers." *Washington Post,* October 20, 1989, p. A18.

Faludi, Susan. "Are the Kids Alright?" *Mother Jones,* November 1988, pp. 15–19.

Fierman, Jaclyn. "Child Care: What Works—And Doesn't." *Fortune,* November 21, 1988, pp. 165–175.

Frankel, Glenn. "Swedish-Made Economic Model May Be Running on Empty." *Washington Post,* March 22, 1990, p. A25.

Friedman, Milton. "Day Care: The Problem." *National Review,* July 8, 1988, p. 14.

Gallagher, Maggie. "Do Congressmen Have Mothers?" *National Review,* October 27, 1989, pp. 38–39, 59.

Galvin, Emily Sedgwick. "Children and Child Care in China: Some Observations." *Children Today,* May/June 1990, pp. 19–23.

Garland, Susan B. "America's Child-Care Crisis: The First Tiny Steps Toward Solutions." *Business Week,* July 10, 1989, pp. 64–68.

Geyelin, Milo. "States Try to Balance Job, Family." *The Wall Street Journal,* May 4, 1990, p. B1.

Gold, Philip. "Bringing Child Care to Work Breaks Home-Office Barriers." *Insight,* March 13, 1989, pp. 40–41.

Guyett, Susan. "Kid Stuff No More." *Indiana Business,* June 1989, pp. 13–18.

Haskins, Ron, and Hank Brown. "The Day-Care Reform Juggernaut." *National Review,* March 10, 1989, pp. 40–41.

Henderson, Nancy. "How to Size Up Day Care." *Changing Times,* July 1988, pp. 69–72.

Hertz, Sue. "Who Cares for the Child?" *Boston Magazine,* March 1989, pp. 124–182.

Hofferth, Sandra L. "What Is the Demand for and Supply of Child Care in the United States?" *Young Children,* July 1989, pp. 28–33.

"IBM Writes the Book on Liberal Leave." *U.S. News & World Report,* October 31, 1988, pp. 13–14.

"Injuries at Day-Care Centers." *Education Week,* October 18, 1989, p. 3.

Jennings, Veronica T. "Studying the Art of Child Care." *Washington Post,* November 30, 1989, p. M1.

Kantrowitz, Barbara, with Pat Wingert and Kate Robins. "Advocating a 'Mommy Track.' " *Newsweek,* March 13, 1989, p. 45.

Klavan, Ellen. "Pick the Best After-School Care." *Parents,* September 1989, pp. 72–82.

Klein, Robert J. "Finding Live-in Help for Your Child That Is Loving, Loyal and Also Legal." *Money,* September 1989, pp. 155–156.

Knight, Robin. "A Euro-solution: Send Toddlers to School." *U.S. News & World Report,* August 22, 1988, pp. 33–36.

Knox, Beverly A., and Donna J. Robinson. "Riverside Medical Center: Everyone's Satisfied." *Management Accounting,* April 1990, pp. 30–31.

Krantz, Paul. "Day Care: Are We Shortchanging Our Kids?" *Better Homes and Gardens,* June 1989, pp. 20–22.

Kreyche, Gerald F. "Day Care: The New Surrogacy." *USA Today* (Magazine), September 1989, pp. 91–93.

La Farge, Phyllis. "A Day in Family Day Care." *Parents,* January 1990, pp. 57–64.

Latimer, Leah Y. "Bringing Up Child Care." *Washington Post,* November, 2, 1989, p. M1.

———"County Seeks a Few Good Day-Care Workers." *Washington Post,* May 10, 1990, p. M1.

———"Sharing Child Care Can Be Illegal Here." *Washington Post,* May 12, 1990, p. D1.

————— "Strict Rules for Day Care Drafted in Md." *Washington Post*, April 5, 1990, p. A1.

Lawson, Carol. "When It Comes to Child Care, French Have a Lesson for U.S." *The New York Times*, p. B1

Lawton, Kim A. "Politicians Discover Children." *Christianity Today*, March 17, 1989, pp. 34–36.

Leslie, Connie, with Karen Springen. "Schools That Never Close." *Newsweek*, May 15, 1989, p. 60.

Levine, James A. "How Employers Are Helping Working Moms." *Good Housekeeping*, September 1990, pp. 150, 192–194.

————— "How Schools Help Families." *Good Housekeeping*, September 1989, pp. 141–142.

Levine, Karen. "Negotiating the Best Parental Leave." *Parents*, May 1989, pp. 74–76.

————— "The Working Mom's Obstacle Course." *Parents*, December 1989, pp. 67–71.

Lewin, Tamar. "Small Tots, Big Biz. *The New York Times Magazine*, January 29, 1989, pp. 30–31, 89–92.

—————. "States' Credits for Child Care Have Little Effect, Study Says." *The New York Times*, November 14, 1989, p. A11.

Long, Lynette. "How Educators Can Help Latchkey Children." *The Education Digest*, March 1989, pp. 53–57.

Mahler, Susan. "Choosing Safe Day Care." *McCall's*, November 1989, p. 62.

Mandel, Susan. "Suffer the Little Children." *National Review*, September 1, 1989, pp. 20–21.

McKuen, Pamela. " 'Substitute Mom' Fills a Need." *Chicago Tribune*, November 7, 1990, p. 64.

Miller, Jim. "Woman's Work Is Never Done." *Newsweek*, July 31, 1989, p. 65.

Nelson, Margaret K. "A Study of Turnover Among Family Day Care Providers." *Children Today*, March/April 1990, pp. 8–12.

Nelson-Harchler, Joani. "Elder Care Comes of Age." *Industry Week*, January 2, 1989, pp. 54–56.

Newman, Cathy. "The Fine Feathered Nest—'La Protection Sociale.'" *National Geographic*, July 1989, pp. 130–131.

Nyborg-Andersen, Irene, and Pamela Guthrie O'Brien. "The Child-Care Patchwork." *Ladies' Home Journal*, November 1989, pp. 199–208.

Polito, Josphine Tutino. "Current Trends in Employer-Supported Childcare." *Early Child Development and Care*, Volume 46 (1989), pp. 39–56.

Reder, Nancy. "Child Care Comes of Age." *The National Voter*, December 1988, pp. 4–9.

Rich, Spencer. "Maternity Leave Benefits Increase." *Washington Post*, April 8, 1990, p. H9.

Roark, Anne C. "Day Care." *Los Angeles Times*, October 31, 1988, Part II, p. 3.

Rodgers, Fran Sussner, and Charles Rodgers. "Business and the Facts of Family Life." *Harvard Business Review*, November/December 1989, pp. 121–129.

Rooks, Judy, "Who's Minding the Kids? More and More It's the Corporation." *The Oregonian*, October 21, 1990, pp. B1, B8.

Rovner, Julie. "Congress Wraps Up Decision on Child-Care Legislation." *Congressional Quarterly*, October 27, 1990, pp. 3605–3606.

Rowell, Sharon. "Mother Load." *The Atlanta Constitution*, May 8, 1990, pp. F1, F4.

Sandroff, Ronni. "Helping Your Company Become Family-Friendly." *Working Woman*, November 1989, pp. 136–139.

Savage, Harlin. "Child Care: The Smart Corporate Investment." *The National Voter*, April/May 1990, pp. 9–11.

Schine, Joan G. "Adolescents Help Themselves by Helping Others." *Children Today*, January/February 1989, pp. 11–15.

Shapiro, Joseph P. "Staff Turnover May Be Day Care's Biggest Problem." *U.S. News & World Report*, October 23, 1989, p. 33.

Shapiro, Joseph P., et al., "When Companies Play Nanny." *U.S. News & World Report*, September 19, 1988, pp. 43–45.

Sheerer, Marilyn, and Paula Jorde-Bloom. "The Ongoing Challenge: Attracting and Retaining Quality Staff." *Child Care Information Exchange*, April 1990, pp. 11–16.

Stern, Loraine. "Day Care: How to Ease Your Worries." *Woman's Day*, July 18, 1989, p. 16.

Sterne, George G., with Barbara Raymond. "Finding the Right Day Care for Your Child!" *Good Housekeeping*, September 1988, pp. 130, 150.

Skrzycki, Cindy. "More Men Taking the Daddy Track." *Washington Post*, November 6, 1990, p. C1.

Taylor, Susan Champlin. "A Promise at Risk." *Modern Maturity*, August/September 1989, pp. 32–41, 84–89.

Teltsch, Kathleen. "For Younger and Older, Workplace Day Care." *The New York Times*, March 10, 1990, p. Y1.

Terpstra, Jake. "Day Care Standards and Licensing." *Child Welfare*, July/August 1989, pp. 437–442.

Tevis, Cheryl. "Who's Watching the Kids?" *Successful Farming*, September 1989, pp. 64–66.

Triedman, Kim. "A Mother's Dilemma." *Ms.*, July/August 1989, pp. 59–63.

Watson, Rita E., and Karen FitzGerald. "21st Century School." *Parents*, October 1989, pp. 112–118.

Weber, Joseph. "Why Day Care Is Still Mostly Mom and Pop." *Business Week,* July 10, 1989, p. 65.

"When It Comes to Child Care, Hospitals May Be Setting the Pace for Much of the Nation." *Journal of the American Medical Association,* April 7, 1989, pp. 1857–1858.

Whitebook, March, et al., "Who Cares? Child Care Teachers and The Quality of Care in America." *Young Children,* November 1989, pp. 41–45.

Wingert, Pat, and Barbara Kantrowitz. "The Day Care Generation." *Newsweek,* Special Issue, Winter/Spring 1990, pp. 86–92.

Wojahn, Ellen. "Bringing Up Baby." *Inc.,* November 1989, pp. 64–75.

Zabell, Martin. "New Child-Care Class Opening Teens' Eyes." *Chicago Tribune,* May 22, 1990, p. 6.

Index